The Ship
That Hunted
Itself

The Ship
That Hunted
Itself ,,

COLIN SIMPSON

STEIN AND DAY/*Publishers*/New York

First published in 1977
Copyright © 1977 by C. & J. Simpson, Ltd.
All rights reserved
Designed by David Miller
Printed in the United States of America
Stein and Day/*Publishers*/Scarborough House,
Briarcliff Manor, N.Y. 10510

Library of Congress Cataloging in Publication Data

Simpson, Colin, 1931-
    The Ship That Hunted Itself

    1. Cap Trafalgar (Steamship) 2. Carmania (Cruiser)
3. European War, 1914-1918—Naval operations, British.
4. European War, 1914-1918—Naval operations, German.
5. European War, 1914-1918—Atlantic Ocean.   I.   Title.
D582.C36S55   940.4′514   76-41888
ISBN 0-8128-1926-8

❥ *Illustrations* ❦

❧ 1 ❧

Toward midnight on August 5, 1914, James Clayton Barr, Captain of the Cunard liner *Carmania,* bade a civil goodnight to his passengers and made his way up to the bridge before turning in. It was a perfect summer night, the air soft, the long Atlantic swell looking warm and inviting as it slipped past. A full moon was glimpsed occasionally through the haze. The *Carmania* was three days out of New York bound for Liverpool with eight hundred passengers and a cargo of bullion valued at $10 million. That evening, despite his responsibilities, James Barr was at peace with the world. He expected to catch the morning tide into Liverpool on August 7, when, after handing over the *Carmania* to a relief captain, he planned a couple of weeks' vacation in Scotland with his family. With luck he would be on the grouse moors when shooting started on the twelfth. He reflected that this would be the first time in his life that he would have both the leisure and the money to be out with the guns on the first day of the season.

He cast a quick, experienced eye over the men on the bridge: the helmsman, the officers of the watch, the motionless figure of a young cadet standing alertly by the engine-room telegraphs. They, in turn, ignored him. His midnight visit was a ritual. They knew that in a moment they would hear the rasp of a match as he lit a forbidden pipe; then as six bells or midnight struck, they would hear a soft "Goodnight, gentle-men" before he went below to his cabin.

Barr crossed to the lee side of the bridge to light his pipe. As he paused, match in hand, he noticed the lights of the British Cruiser H.M.S. *Bristol*, about a mile away and steaming a parallel course. *Bristol* had appeared earlier in the day, but, apart from an exchange of courtesy signals, had ignored them. Barr cupped his hands, bent down and lit his pipe. When he straightened up, the *Bristol* had disappeared.

Barr thought he had lost his night vision for a moment; the flare of a match played that kind of trick. He strained his eyes across the dark water, but could see nothing. He reasoned that if the cruiser's power had failed her auxiliary generators would restore it in a moment. Nevertheless, a caution bred by years of command prompted him to grunt the order "Reduce to half speed." His order, repeated first by the watchkeeper, then by the cadet on the telegraph, was acknowledged by a call from the engine room. In the silence, Barr could hear his engineer officer's voice echoing up the voice pipe and across the bridge. "What's up? Has the old man dropped that bloody pipe overboard?"

Barr remained silent. He was calculating speeds and distances. Somewhere on his port beam was several thousand tons of steel, without lights and keeping station with him—or was it? In a few moments, the *Bristol* had changed from a friendly, bright-lit, and reassuring presence to a collision hazard. At that moment, the moon broke through the haze and highlighted the bow wave of the *Bristol*, which was closing fast with the *Carmania*. Barr leaped for the siren lanyard and sounded off the international signal "You are steering into danger"; then just as he was about to order full speed and hard-a-starboard, the *Bristol*, using engines as well as rudder, turned sharply so that she broadsided almost alongside him, her engines creaming the water between the

8

two ships into a mass of phosphorescence. Then a megaphone boomed across from the warship. *"Carmania,* war is declared—darken ship—radio silence."

Barr had hardly time to acknowledge before the *Bristol* accelerated away into the night, and as if in sympathy with the signal, the moon slipped again behind the cloud. Once *Bristol's* order had been carried out to his satisfaction, Barr ordered resumption of normal cruising speed, and went below.

In the quietness of his cabin he opened his safe, taking out his log book, his personal diary, and a sealed envelope, which was endorsed, "Only to be opened in the event of hostilities." He quickly entered the war signal in the log, then opened his sealed instructions. As he had expected, the *Carmania* was to be handed over to the Admiralty as soon as she reached port. It was an open secret among Cunard captains that the company had borrowed several million pounds from the British Government in exchange for the promise that, in wartime, Cunard ships would become armed cruisers. The *Carmania's* decks even had mounting rings for eight 4.7-inch guns built into them. As far as he could see, his remaining responsibility was to take his ship safely into Liverpool and hand her over. Picking up the intercom, he called the bridge, ordered double lookouts to be posted, and sent a sleepy party from the duty watch to check that all the lifeboats were provisioned with water and food and that the davits were properly greased. Then he picked up his diary and noted the declaration of war. As an afterthought he added, "Thank God I was never taught to hate any man."

James Barr was then in his sixtieth year. He had gone to sea before the mast in 1877. Before graduating to steam and joining Cunard, he had been shipwrecked three times. His early years had been in the South America trade, and almost every voyage had involved rounding Cape Horn. Once he had joined Cunard, promotion had come quickly, and before the *Carmania* he had commanded several of the company's better-known liners, including the *Mauretania.* In peacetime, he could expect another couple of years at sea, then promotion to Senior Commodore, acting as relief captain when occasion demanded until he retired at sixty-five. "Commodore of the Line" had been his ambition, but he realized that evening that, with most of Cunard's ships in Admiralty hands, there would be neither need nor ships for his future services.

He was, he believed, too old to be considered for active service. Besides, he had little taste for the Royal Navy. During the Boer War he had been in command of the *Catalonia,* which had been requisitioned by the Admiralty. To his disgust, she had been turned into a floating prison camp for captured Boers. Characteristically he had not kept his disgust to himself, and he knew that admirals, like elephants, never forget. He saw little chance that he would be offered any position of responsibility. Besides, he rather liked the Germans. In fact he had been especially taken with the young naval officer who had traveled with him on the outward voyage to New York. What was his name? He turned up the diary, Korvette Kapitän Müller. Surely he had had no idea of the impending war. What was it he had said? He had noted it down. "Your nation and mine are like rival shopkeepers, each trying to sell their own wares. As for anything else—it is unthinkable."

At breakfast next morning, Barr made a point of talking to as many passengers as possible. Usually he took the meal in his own quarters, but today he felt that there would be many wanting reassurance. He moved among them with a jocularity he did not feel, explaining that the extra lifeboat drills he had ordered were a routine precaution, that the *Bristol* was still lurking beyond the horizon, apologizing to irate businessmen that he could not break radio silence to send their cables. One passenger's question touched him on the raw. "I suppose, Captain," she gushed, "you will be placed in command of a warship immediately we arrive in England." Barr stiffened, then answered with as much sincerity as he could muster. "Quite impossible, ma'am. I'm shooting on the twelfth."

In 1914, the London edition of the *Times* reached Zürich around noon the day after publication. It took almost as long again to travel the thirty miles to the Pension Schmidt in the little resort of Cluses high on the St. Bernard Pass. The issue of Saturday, August 1, 1914, was further delayed by the devotions of the Swiss on the Sabbath. When a copy eventually arrived, it was handed to a middle-aged man who was watching the sunset from a deck chair with a rug tucked over his knees. Beside him sat a young woman, surrounded by the paraphernalia of a nurse. She waited silently while her companion scanned the paper. "I want," he said, "I want to go home at once. Please arrange everything so that we leave tomorrow morning."

The nurse, who was called Elspeth Fairlie, knew better than to argue. The invalid was her cousin Noel Grant, already at the age of forty-five a full Captain in the Royal Navy, and plagued by what he called "this damned asthma." Elspeth was well aware that this was a euphemism for tuberculosis but would never have dreamed of saying so. Sometimes she wondered if Noel really knew the truth, and she privately thought it a crime that the Royal Navy persisted in calling it asthma. Tuberculosis was pensionable, asthma was not. For a family that was chronically short of money and that had scrimped and saved to get Noel into the Navy, every penny was important.

Noel Grant had joined the Navy as a boy. At the age of sixteen he had graduated at the top of his class on the H.M.S.

Britannia training ship and by sheer hard work had risen to his present rank in under twenty years. This was a formidable achievement for anyone. For an officer without patronage or private means and, unhappily, totally devoid of charm, it was a miracle. Noel's formula had been to make himself absolutely indispensable. He knew every instruction manual, rulebook, and naval regulation by heart. He was an expert navigator, was regarded as a foremost authority on pilotage in West Indian waters, and had a reputation as a strict disciplinarian. He had a total grasp of his job, numerous commendations for efficiency, and remarkably few friends.

His career had been dogged by ill health. Whenever he had been given a command, his health had let him down, even though it was widely recognized that his ships were superbly run. The *Terror,* the *Sapphire,* and the *Irresistible* had been unbeatable under him, admittedly at a time when the yardstick for comparison was the discipline and appearance of the crew, the way the ships records and accounts were kept, the gloss of the paint, the gleam of the brasswork. He had never seen active service of any kind and spent his leaves on lonely sketching holidays, usually with his mother, and lately with his cousin Elspeth.

In November, 1913, his health had given the Admiralty serious concern, and he was asked to relinquish his command and take a year's leave on half pay. Instead, he applied for three months' sick leave on full pay. This was refused. The difference in pay would have meant proper medical treatment, which he wished to obtain privately in Switzerland, probably to keep the real nature of his illness from his superiors. There was a secondary reason for being abroad. A few months earlier he had been named as corespondent in a divorce case involving a fellow officer, Commander Vaughan. In those days, divorce carried a social stigma and did not further a career. After a divorce, the lady concerned was not free to marry under English law for a period of six months.

During the first six months of 1914, he had watched the war clouds gather over Europe from his deck chair in the Alps, and now, after reading that both the British and German navies were under full mobilization, he saw it as his duty to return home at once. Noel Grant scented the war he had trained for, which could restore him to full-pay status and possible promotion. It was one short step to rear admiral, and admirals did not suffer the indignity either of being on the beach or of half pay, or both combined. If they were unfit, then it was an honorable and pensionable retirement. Shortly after noon on August 5, Captain Noel Grant, R.M., reported to the Admiralty in London that he was fit for active service. In the confusion of the time he was not asked to have a medical examination.

While Captains Barr and Grant headed their separate ways toward England, a far stranger journey was in progress. Deep in the South Atlantic, a thousand miles west of Cape Town, His Imperial German Majesty's gunboat *Eber* plugged further west. A mile or two astern of her, a small coastal steamer followed in her wake. Both were rust streaked and had seen considerably better days. The *Eber*'s natural habitat was the estuaries, rivers, and lakes of German West Africa. The *Steiemark*, for that was the steamer's name, had been nearing the end of a grubby, if honest, career serving the settlements along the African coast. The South Atlantic was not their natural element, and both the ships and their crews were uncomfortably aware of it.

The crew of the *Steiemark* were especially bewildered. A week previously they had been peacefully at anchor in Lüderitz Bay. The *Eber* had come alongside, the Captain had come aboard, placed them under martial law, ordered them to take on as much coal and provisions as she could carry, and to follow him. They had coal not only in the holds but in the passages on the decks, even in part of the crew's quarters. To add to their confusion and discomfort, the lifeboats contained a motley assortment of pigs, chickens, and goats.

They had no idea of their destination, and as they were forbidden to use the radio, were ignorant as to the reason why. They relied for that on the *Eber*'s Captain.

Korvette Kapitän Julius Wirth had a shrewd suspicion of what he was up to. On July 30, he had been with the *Eber* in Cape Town, seeking some essential spare parts for his engine room, when the local German consul had brought him a cable from the German Admiralty ordering him to proceed immediately to Lüderitz Bay. On his arrival there, he received further instructions ordering a general mobilization of the German Navy and placing him on a war footing. He was ordered to take on as much coal and supplies as he could carry, requisition any seaworthy German ship in the vicinity, and load her up as well. He was then to sail on a west northwesterly course as far out to sea as possible and await further orders.

From southwestern Africa, a west northwesterly course meant home to Germany. Captain Wirth saw his mission as taking his tiny little ship and supplies back home, though he must have wondered exactly what contribution one estuary gunboat would make to the German Navy, even assuming he managed to dodge the British fleet guarding the English Channel. His ship, the *Eber*, was built for operations in the tropics. She had a shallow draft and, in anything like a sea, rolled like a pig. She carried a puny armament of two 4.1-inch guns and six machine guns, all of some vintage, and apart from the occasional firing practice never used. His ammunition tended to deteriorate in the tropics, and he had had to report that at practice it frequently failed to explode.

✎ ❧

Julius Wirth was thirty-eight and immensely proud of his command. Like Captain Grant he had joined the Navy as a boy and had done well. His record of service shows him to have been regarded as an outstanding officer, likely to rise high in the Navy. By rights he should have been, according to his qualifications, the second in command of a modern battle cruiser. All his experience had been in large men of war. It is a mystery why he was employed as the Captain of a rusty old-fashioned river gunboat in one of the remotest backwaters of the German colonial empire. Possibly it was because he wished to command, or that he was trying to save money. He certainly came from a modest family, and career officers in the German Navy usually needed a private income of their own to supplement their pay. It is unlikely that his current appointment stemmed from prejudice, as German records show that he had volunteered for the assignment.

He certainly enjoyed himself in West Africa. He was free to do almost exactly what he pleased. His presence there was merely to "show the flag." There were no pirates to fight or rebellions to put down. There was the occasional chase after diamond smugglers and frequent enjoyable leaves in Cape Town, where the leaky and ramshackle old *Eber* was a constant visitor for repairs. His crew regarded him with respect and affection. Their letters from the *Eber* still exist in the German Naval archives and are rich with phrases such as "Our wonderful Captain," "Our beloved Captain."

Since leaving the African coast, the *Eber* had maintained radio silence, but each evening she listened in at a prearranged time. On August 5, she received a coded signal ordering her to "rendezvous with other units" at the remote island of Trinidad deep in the South Atlantic. This is not to be confused with the large island of the same name in the West Indies. It is a lofty and rocky uninhabited outcrop, four miles long by two broad, 617 miles east of the Brazilian coast. Wirth had neither charts nor experience of those waters, but he had the precise latitude and longitude, 20° 30′ south and 29° 30′ west. Signaling the *Steiemark* to follow him, he altered course and, using compass, sextant, and dead reckoning, headed for the rendezvous.

He arrived off Trinidad in the early evening of August 15. Waiting for him he found four small colliers, all as heavily loaded as the *Steiemark*. He called the masters of the colliers together and, in the absence of any other instructions, took command of the tiny fleet, ordering landing parties onto the island to check that it was uninhabited and to post lookouts on the highest point. Then he reloaded his own bunkers and began a cautious patrol a few miles off shore. He dared not use his radio, for the air was thick with the signals of British warships. Toward dawn he sighted the dim outline of a cruiser, and was mightily relieved to find it was the modern German cruiser *Dresden*. Cruiser and gunboat anchored together a half mile off the island and Captain Wirth, trying to make himself as presentable as possible, went aboard.

The two ships must have presented an incongruous sight. The *Eber*'s tropical white paintwork was streaked with rust and coal dust. Her afterdeck was covered with a tattered awning, the poles of which had been hastily wired around to make a chicken run. Her pumps chattered away, spewing rusty water from her bilges, for her plates had been badly strained during the crossing. While the *Dresden* sat majestically motionless in the light swell, the little *Eber* bobbed up and down like a cork. Captain Wirth must have felt rather incongruous himself as he was piped aboard, saluted by a marine escort, and taken down to the Captain's cabin.

After congratulating him on his passage, Captain Lüdecke told him that very shortly an armed cruiser would be arriving, and that he was to assume command. In the meantime, he was to remain at Trinidad, guard the colliers from marauding

British cruisers, and maintain strict radio silence. He was given a set of recognition signals so that he could identify which were friendly ships by day or night, and then was asked if there was anything that he wanted.

"A very remarkable young officer," Lüdecke was to write later. "All he asked for was some ice and vegetables for his crew, charts, paint, and machine-gun ammunition for his ship, and permission to send his men aboard in parties so that they could bathe and use the laundry. I agreed and pressed him if there was anything else. He blushed like a schoolboy and asked if *Dresden*'s tailor shop could run him up a battle ensign of the German Navy, his own was a tattered wisp as he had flown it all the way from Africa."

The S.S. *Cap Trafalgar* was the pride, joy, and flagship of the Hamburg South America Line. She had been completed shortly before the outbreak of war and had just completed her maiden voyage. When war was declared, she lay anchored alongside the passenger terminal at Buenos Aires, towering over every other ship in the port. She was a triple-screw turbine vessel with a reputed speed of eighteen knots. Her seven-hundred-foot length was painted a deep blue, her upperworks, a dazzling white. These sported a rash of gaily striped blue-and-white awnings, which covered the swimming pool and badminton courts on her foredeck. Her bridge, which was open to the elements, was railed in polished teak and also covered by a canvas awning. Abaft of three immense funnels was her after superstructure, which was unique in that it was largely of glass. This was called the Winter Garden and comprised a series of terraces laid in yellow marble. These were interplanted with banks of tropical plants and flowers. Fountains played while myriads of tropical birds, parrots, macaws, and toucanets, chattered and displayed from a series of perches and cleverly designed cages.

The roof of the Winter Garden was supported on a range of classical pillars. Part of it slid back in the tropics, but in temperate climates the interior gave passengers the impression that, on boarding the ship, they were stepping straight into a Mayan temple, set in a tropical paradise.

The *Cap Trafalgar* was commanded by Kommandant Fritz Langerhannsz, a tall, distinguished man who was the senior captain of his company. He was a sophisticated internationalist, fluent in several languages, a polo player and a yachtsman of international class. He had gone to sea relatively late in life, having taken a modern-language degree at Heidelberg and studied architecture in London. A love of sailing had led him into naval architecture, and from there it had been a natural progression to the German merchant marine. He was equally at home in Germany, South America, or Great Britain, particularly the latter, for he was a frequent guest and a competitor at Cowes.

The *Cap Trafalgar* was a very apt ship for Langerhannsz to command for yet another reason. Her name evoked Nelson and had in fact been deliberately chosen to attract English passengers to travel in her to South America. Langerhannsz was a formidable Nelson scholar. He had translated Southey's two-volume biography into German and had supervised the decoration of the smoking room and the library with a wide selection of pictures showing Nelson's major exploits, while innumerable portraits of the little English admiral decorated many of the rooms. The deluxe cabins or suites were named after the British and French men of war engaged in the Battle of Trafalgar, while the names of Nelson's contemporaries were constantly appearing on the various confections dreamed up by the chefs. Hardy, Hope, Blackwood, and Collingwood were best known to passengers on the *Cap Trafalgar* as the names of ice creams.

She had arrived at Buenos Aires on August 2, after a

leisurely maiden voyage from Hamburg, calling on the way at Southampton in order to show many of his English yachting acquaintances around his new ship. Langerhannsz had openly discussed the threat of war with them. Mr. Winston Churchill had recently announced in Parliament that the conversion of several British liners to armed cruisers had been completed in order to protect Britain's trade routes. Langerhannsz conceded it was true that the Hamburg South America Line had also drawn a subsidy from the German Government and, in exchange, built steel mounting rings into the decks so that she could be armed in a hurry. Pointing to the Winter Garden, Langerhannsz had joked that "people in glass houses would be exceptionally foolish to start throwing stones."

After landing his passengers, he commenced to discharge cargo. He was watching the operations from the bridge when the German Consul arrived at the ship to tell him that Germany was at war with England. He asked Langerhannsz if he had any orders, and, if not, what his intentions were. Langerhannsz told him that he had no orders as to what to do in the event of war and that he was due to sail back to Hamburg with a full complement of passengers on August 10. The *Cap Trafalgar* was a passenger ship, she was unarmed, and he could see no earthly reason why the English should stop him. If the international situation made returning to Germany impossible, then he would coal and sail his ship to the United States, where the line had an American-registered company. There he would suggest that the ship be reregistered under the American flag and continue the South America run operating out of an American port. The Consul, telling him not to sail until he received further instructions, went ashore to report back to Berlin.

That evening, the Consul called a meeting of all the captains of German ships in the port. He said that the German Admiralty had ordered that no one was to leave, with the exception that one of them would run the gauntlet of the British Fleet in an attempt to take reservists and those who wished to volunteer to fight back to Germany. He also asked them to discharge from their crews all those who were not of German nationality. Lastly, he asked them to ensure that they were all fully bunkered with coal, water, and provisions, to keep their crews aboard ship, and to avoid any conflicts with Allied seamen who might be in the port. Similar instructions were issued by the British and French consulates to the masters of ships flying their respective flags.

Buenos Aires was considerably influenced by the British community. Argentina imported most of her coal from England, and in those days coal meant electric power and energy for much of Argentine industry. Immediately after war was declared, a fuel panic swept the country, and at first the government forbade any ship of any nationality to take on coal. After assurances from the British Foreign Office that Britain would continue to export Argentina's requirements, the President rescinded the refueling embargo, but at the same time, the British gained the diplomatic initiative. This was followed up by a virulent anti-German press campaign urging suppliers not to deal with their German customers.

Langerhannsz had his work cut out trying to obtain the supplies he needed. He had lost more than a hundred members of his crew, who planned to return to Germany, including, to his chagrin, his head chef, four of his officers, his personal steward, and the bird keeper who tended the Winter Garden. With considerable charm, he persuaded most of the members of the ship's orchestra to double up in the stokehold and, to use as fuel in lieu of coal, managed to purchase a consignment of one thousand railway ties, which he stowed wherever he could. Three hundred that he could not squeeze down below he stacked along the boat deck. He was determined to take his ship out on time, and no navy, British or German, was going to stop him.

Noel Grant had reported to the Admiralty on August 5. To his delight he had been accepted for active service and asked to report daily. The following morning he was told that he had been appointed to command the *Carmania* and that she was due at Liverpool at dawn the following day. He was to meet her, formally requisition her, supervise her conversion, and prepare for active service. The *Carmania*'s armament was already waiting for her in Liverpool. In fact it had been delivered to Cunard the previous March.

Captain Grant was to be supported by the services of Lieutenant Commander E. Lockyer, a retired career naval officer living in Portsmouth, who would be his gunnery officer. Commander Lockyer would bring with him thirty-eight Royal Marines to act as gunners and to provide an infantry party for boarding purposes. The Admiralty regretted that they could not spare any more officers to assist him, but pointed out that most of the *Carmania*'s civilian officers were members of the Royal Naval Reserve and therefore could be kept on the ship. Captain Grant was to report his crew requirements as soon as possible. The Admiralty trusted that he would be able to persuade many of her peacetime crew to volunteer.

There was just one snag as far as Grant was concerned. He had never held command of a ship as large as the *Carmania*, and twenty years ago in 1894 he had faced a board of inquiry for grounding his ship. He had been exonerated, but the Admiralty, ever cautious, hesitated before putting him in charge of a ship displacing 20,000 tons, 675 feet long, and when fully laden drawing 44 feet. He was formally instructed that he was to offer her present master, Captain Barr, the opportunity to sail with him as "adviser," and to make matters easier for Captain Barr, or perhaps to make it harder for him to refuse the invitation, Grant was handed the formal document appointing Barr a temporary commander in the Royal Naval Reserve.

He had it with him when he arrived at Cunard's Liverpool

dock shortly before 8 A.M. the following morning. The official history of the Cunard Company tells what happened then with admirable brevity.

Carmania docked at Liverpool landing stage at 8 o'clock in the morning of August 7th 1914. She was almost immediately boarded by Captain Noel Grant, R.M., and Lieutenant-Commander E. Lockyer, R.M., who were to be respectively her Captain and First Lieutenant under the new conditions. At that moment she looked about as unlike a man-of-war as she could well have done. From half a dozen gangways, baggage was being landed at express speed, while first and second class passengers were also going ashore from the overhead gantries. Owing to the fact that there were known to be Germans amongst the passengers on board, a considerable number of police and custom officials were present upon the vessel; and this necessitated the detention of a large number of third-class passengers, who had to be carefully scrutinized and sorted out.

While all this was going on, arrangements for the equipment and personnel of the vessel were already being discussed, and the proportions of Cunarders and Naval ratings for the *Carmania*'s future war service being determined. It was decided that the engine staff was to be Cunard, the men being specially enrolled for a period of six months in the Royal Naval Reserve, while the Commander of the Ship, Captain J. C. Barr, was to remain on board as navigator and advisor to Captain Grant, with the temporary rank of Commander R.N.R. The Chief Officer, Lieutenant Murchie, with certain other officers, also remained on board, Lieutenant Murchie, owing to his special knowledge of the ship ranking next to Lieutenant-Commander Lockyer for general working purposes. The ship's surgeon, her chief steward, and about 50 of the Cunard ratings for cooks, waiters, and officers' servants were also retained, as well as the carpenter, who was kept on board as Chief Petty Officer and given six mates. The cooper, blacksmith, plumber, and painter being also retained with the same rank.

Leaving the stage about noon, the *Carmania* was immediately docked at Sandon, where after some further delay the third-class passengers were landed. Owing to the fact that the *Carmania* was already in the *Carmania's* proper berth, being fitted out as an armed cruiser, and that both she and the *Aquitania* were already well on the way to completion for their new task, the *Carmania* could for the moment neither discharge her cargo nor bunker, owing to the shortage of labor. As many painters, however, as could be assembled began at once to alter her hull and funnels, blackening out her well-known red and black tops, while a gang of shipwrights started to cut out the bulwarks fore and aft on the 'B' deck, in order to allow of the training to suitable angles of the guns that were to be placed in position there. Other Cunard stewards and joiners concentrated at once upon the task of clearing out passenger accommodation from the vessel. During Saturday and Sunday the *Carmania* remained in the basin. On Monday she was able to get an empty berth, where she began at once to discharge her cargo, and to bunker at express speed. Armored plates were now being put in position upon all her most vulnerable parts, and these were also re-inforced with coal and bags of sand by way of extra protection. All the woodwork in the passengers' quarters were taken away; two of her holds were being fitted with platforms, and magazines were being built on them; while means for flooding were also being installed, speaking-tubes were fitted in the aft steering gear room, control telephones being run up, and her eight guns placed in position.

These were all of 4.7 inch calibre and with a range of about 9,300 yards. In addition a 6 foot Barr and Stroud range-finder was being fitted, together with two semaphores. Two search-lights were being mounted on slightly raised platforms on the bridge ends, while two ordinary lifeboats and eighteen Maclean collapsible boats were retained for war purposes. By Wednesday all the coal was in, all the bunkers being full, and the protection coal was in place. At 5 o'clock the next morning, the detachment of naval ratings arrived from Portsmouth, most of them being R.N.R. men, but a good many belonging to the Royal Fleet Reserve, while the Marines on board were drawn in equal proportions from the Royal Marine Artillery, and the Royal Marine Light Infantry. The able seamen were for the most part Scotch fishermen of the finest type. ·

On the same day messing, watch, and sleeping arrangements were made, ammunition was taken aboard and stored in the magazines, together with a limited number of small arms, in addition to the marines' rifles: and so unremitting had been the work of all engaged, and so efficient the organization evoked by the crisis that the *Carmania* was actually at sea as a fully equipped armed cruiser by Friday, August 14th, only a week after she had entered port as an ordinary first-class Atlantic liner.

The speed and efficiency with which the *Carmania* and numerous other ships were converted was not matched by the Germans. They had long had contingency plans to utilize their larger liners as armed marauding cruisers, but the detailed execution of those plans went seriously wrong. When war broke out, Germany had planned to have forty-two armed liners in commission within a week. In fact, she had none.

On August 1, when the full mobilization of the German Fleet had been ordered, Admiral Tirpitz had requested the German Government to send out immediately into the international trade routes merchantmen that Germany already possessed. The Kaiser had ignored his request. Incredible as it may seem, Admiral Tirpitz, who was the German Naval Secretary of State, was completely cut off from the tactical and strategical control of his command. This isolation was so complete that, as he conceded in his memoirs, he did not even know the German Navy's war plans.

The unfortunate Tirpitz found himself relegated to fulfilling a purely administrative role, and had been moved, together with his staff, to an annex of the Kaiser's suite at General Headquarters. The Kaiser would discuss naval matters only through his favorite, the Naval Chief of Staff, von Pohl, who regarded Tirpitz as a rival and did his best to keep him at arm's length. Von Pohl's staff naturally echoed their chief's attitude and resisted all Tirpitz's attempts to seek the Kaiser's ear. As a result, and in Tirpitz's own account, the operational staff of the German Navy was gripped by a total state of paralysis for the first few months of the war.

At the end of August, 1914, the British Admiralty was to announce rather smugly that of Germany's forty-two liners that she had planned to arm and then use to molest Britain's supply routes, seventeen were bottled up in neutral harbors with British warships maintaining a constant blockade outside. At the outbreak of war, fourteen were moored in Germany, where the impotent Tirpitz was still fighting with von Pohl to obtain the release of the armament with which he planned to equip them, while a further six had been seized by the British as they had tried to escape from ports under British control at the outbreak of war. This left five, of which only one, the *Kaiser Wilhelm der Grosse,* was armed. However, she had the misfortune to encounter the British cruiser *Highflyer* on August 26, 1914, and was speedily dispatched. This left the *Kronprinz Wilhelm,* which was surprised off the American coast in the act of having armament transferred from the *Karlsruhe* on the morning of August 6. Unable to put up a fight, she relied on superior speed to escape into the Atlantic, where, short of coal and with only half her planned armament aboard, she was dependent on either capturing an Allied collier or rendezvousing with a friendly one before she could prove much of a menace.

Of the remaining three, the *Santa Isabel* remained unarmed but managed to slip out of Buenos Aires on August 9 with a cargo of bullocks, coal, sandbags, and shovels. The *Baden* was employed as an unarmed tender to the cruiser *Dresden* and the *Cap Trafalgar.* The British Admiralty decided to concentrate on the *Cap Trafalgar*, which, as the largest, fastest, and potentially the most damaging vessel, they decided was to be prevented from making her escape into the supply routes at all costs.

While the *Cap Trafalgar* lay moored in Buenos Aires awaiting her orders, the *Baden* and the *Santa Isabel* lurked off Trinidad Island, awaiting the *Dresden* and *Eber*. Scouring the South Atlantic for them were the British warships *Invincible, Carnavon, Cornwall, Kent, Glasgow, Bristol, Defence, Albion, Minotaur, Weymouth,* and *Dartmouth,* each one of which, even if the German ships had been fully equipped with their full armament as planned, could have sunk her opponent without coming into range of the German guns.

The almost incredible state of preparedness of the British Navy had been due to the foresight of the British First Lord of the Admiralty, Winston Churchill. He had foreseen war with Germany the previous year, and during 1914, instead of ordering the annual fleet maneuvers that traditionally culminated in a massive display of naval strength off some fashionable seaside resort to impress foreign observers and be reviewed by the King, followed by maneuver leave for the men and a spectacular series of balls and social functions, Churchill had ordered a test mobilization. First- and second-line reserve categories were called up, joined their ships, and spent two weeks training as for war. This test mobilization ended on July 25. However, only second-line reservists were sent home and the regular "maneuver leave" was cancelled.

On July 28, Churchill decided to commit the Royal Navy to full combat readiness. His naval staff agreed, but the Cabinet, had it been asked, would have vetoed the suggestion. They had already bitterly criticized the test mobilization. Taking only the Prime Minister into his confidence, Churchill, on his own initiative, sent the Navy to its battle stations, armed, fueled, and with its full fighting complement of men aboard. There was at the time, and there are today, critics who aver this was saber rattling of the highest order, but when at 11 P.M. London time on August 4, 1914, England entered a state of war with Germany, the Royal Navy, wherever it was, had been on full combat alert for almost a week, and so had the unseen eyes and ears of the Admiralty in every corner of the world.

๏2๏

As Britain was the main supplier of coal to the South American countries, it had been only natural that the Hamburg South America Line had traditionally placed its bunkering contracts with British colliers. These little ships, normally laden with Welsh steam coal, made the regular run down the South American east coast ports, and the German Coal Company, Ltd., of 228 Boulevard Maipu, Buenos Aires, was a valued customer. On the first morning of the war, the master of the Swansea-registered collier *Daffodil,* berthed in Buenos Aires, received the following formal letter from Mr. H. C. Mackie, the British Consul General in the port.

Buenos Aires,
5th August, 1914.

Sir,

It has been brought to my notice that you are engaged in discharging coal for the German Coal Co., at Maipu 288, while it is known that this coal is being shipped on the German S.S. *Cap Trafalgar.*

Coal, when supplied to a hostile war vessel, is contraband of war, and renders the purveyor liable to heavy penalties.

In this case the *Cap Trafalgar* is not ostensibly a war vessel, but it is believed on good grounds to be capable of conversion into an armed cruiser and there are various reasons for considering that such conversion will take place after the ship leaves port.

It is also highly probable that part of the coal carried is destined for German men-of-war. There is good reason, therefore, that the supplying of coal in such circumstances amounts to a constructive offence against the law of contraband.

In these circumstances, I have to request you to desist from supplying coal until instructions are received from H.B.M. Government.

> I remain, Sir,
> Your obedient Servant
> H. G. Mackie
> H.M. Consul-General.

The Commander S.S. *Daffodil*

In this way, Mr. Mackie's well-intentioned and patriotic note started the train of events that undoubtedly caused both the Foreign Office and Admiralty in London to view the actions of the *Cap Trafalgar* and the Argentine authorities with the gravest suspicion. Mackie dutifully sent a copy of his letter to Mr. Norman, the British Chargé d'Affaires, who in turn telegraphed a detailed report to Sir Edward Grey, the British Foreign Secretary in London. Norman's telegram, despite its stilted language, amply confirms that the Admiralty's instructions to thwart Tirpitz's plans were afoot *before* Germany mobilized on August 1 and casts some light on the diplomatic principles that Britain was seeking to impose upon neutrals.

The main point was that if any neutral country materially assisted a combatant ship by supplying coal, provisions, etc. then, if that ship at some future date should in any way destroy or damage British property, Britain would hold the neutral country at least partially responsible and seek com-

pensation, backed up by diplomatic and commercial sanc-
tions. It was a philosophy to which the Argentines did not take
kindly.

No. 115.

Buenos Aires,
August 5th 1914.

Sir,

On receipt of your telegram of yesterday informing me that
Great Britain was at war with Germany and instructing me to act as
previously directed, I lost no time in addressing to the Argentine
Minister for Foreign Affairs an urgent Note relative to the arming of
belligerent merchant vessels in neutral ports in accordance with the
terms of your Telegram No. 7 of the 29th. ultimo.

I followed up my Note by calling on His Excellency this
afternoon and in the course of our interview explained to him the
principle at stake, with which he appeared to be quite unfamiliar.

I was able to illustrate my argument by the concrete case of the
German steamer *Cap Trafalgar* of the Hamburg South America line,
now lying in this port.

In consequence of rumors which recently reached him with
regard to this vessel, His Majesty's Consul General at this Capital
had her proceedings watched and is convinced that she has on
board, besides guns with which to assist her own conversion into a
cruiser, spare guns which she is gradually transferring to other
German merchantmen in the port under cover of the night, no
doubt with a similar object.

Mr. Mackie is also in possession of trustworthy evidence that the
guns in question have actually been seen on board the vessel.

I pointed out to the Minister that these proceedings of the *Cap
Trafalgar* constituted a manifest violation of Argentine neutrality
and that to permit their continuance was inconsistent with the duty

of this Republic, as a neutral nation, towards a friendly Power and I accordingly urged His Excellency to take without delay the necessary steps to put a stop to them.

His Excellency promised to make immediate inquiries into the matter.

I told the French Minister this morning of the instructions which I had received from you regarding the arming of belligerent vessels in neutral ports and also discussed with him the proceedings of the *Cap Trafalgar* which are now publicly discussed all over the town.

He expressed the intention of making identical representations on these two points and did so this afternoon.

Norman's telegram provoked an immediate response in London. Apart from the diplomatic principles it involved, it confirmed that the *Cap Trafalgar* was actively being prepared for a combatant role. Naval Intelligence decided that her role would be to slip to sea, and then team up with the German cruiser *Dresden.* They believed that they were unlikely to remain in South American waters, and visualized them moving eastward, where they would wreak havoc on British transports coming from Cape Town, and possibly bolster German resistance in Southwest Africa.

Even as Norman's telegram was being analyzed, the Argentine Foreign Minister was replying to Norman in no uncertain terms. His reply, dated August 6, placed Norman in a difficult position:

TRANSLATION

Ministry for Foreign Affairs and Public Worship	Buenos Aires, August 6, 1914.

ARGENTINE REPUBLIC

Monsieur le Chargé d'Affaires,

I have received your Note of this day's date in which you inform me that, according to information received by His Britannic Majesty's Consul General from a trustworthy source, spare guns have been found on board the S.S. *Cap Trafalgar,* moored in the port of Buenos Aires, and that the operation of transferring them to other German vessels, under cover of the night, has been observed by witnesses worthy of credit.

The Argentine Government, with a view to observing the strictest neutrality between the Nations which are in a state of war, had issued, before the receipt of your Note, the necessary instructions that vessels moored in the port should be inspected and that any operations tending to equip them for war purposes should be prevented. From the investigations made by the proper authorities and from the result of the watch kept by them during the last few days, it appears that there are no arms on board the *Cap Trafalgar* and that no operations of transfer have been noticed.

The examination embraced the whole vessel, with the exception of two holds not yet unloaded, the contents of which will be inspected as they are discharged. In any case if there had been arms on board it would not have been possible to see them as declared by His Britannic Majesty's Consul General.

Owing to the contradiction which exists between these reports and the statements contained in your Note, I hastened to request you orally during our interview today to support your assertion in order that the proper inquiry might be held.

I repeat now this request, asking you to state the names of the witnesses mentioned in your Note, as the vagueness of the term employed in it does not allow of the elucidation of the matter.

I avail myself, etc.

(Signed) José Luis Murature

Norman was being asked to "put up or shut up." He took his time about what he should do and omitted to inform

London what had transpired until August 17, by which time a squadron of the Royal Navy was lying in wait for the *Cap Trafalgar*. After informing Sir Edward Grey of the peremptory demand for evidence from the Argentines he continued:

... It seemed at first sight easy to comply with this demand, but it has proved in the event, to be quite impossible, either because the persons who made the assertions are too timid to substantiate them, or because, in making them, they were drawing on their imagination.

In these somewhat embarrassing circumstances, I consulted the French Minister who has been some years in this country, and who was conversant with the question, having made joint representations on the subject with myself on the 5th instant.

Monsieur Jullemier showed no astonishment at the failure to induce the authors of these positive assertions to confirm them by sworn declarations, and with his concurrence I have now addressed to Dr. Murature a further Note explaining the circumstances.

Neither M. Jullemier, Mr. Mackie nor I have any doubt that the *Cap Trafalgar* has guns and ammunition on board, of which the fact, mentioned to me by Dr. Murature himself, that she had gun platforms, appears to furnish sufficient proof, and I am convinced that the action which I took, if somewhat precipitate, has had the desired effect of preventing the vessel from carrying out any designs which she may have had of converting herself into a cruiser either on the high seas or in this neutral port.

I was agreeably surprised at the promptitude with which the Argentine Authorities, even before the receipt of my Note of the 6th, proceeded to the examination of the vessel, since my previous experience of the dilatoriness of their methods had not prepared me for such an exhibition of zeal, but I am far from satisfied of the efficiency of the search which they made on board her.

In this connection I would invite your attention to the penultimate paragraph of a letter addressed to Mr. Mackie by the Master of the French steamer *Lutétia* which was then berthed next to the *Cap Trafalgar*.

I may remark that the Master is an Officer who belongs to the French Navy seconded for the purpose of commanding the vessel and may therefore be supposed to know something of the way in which a search for guns should be conducted.

I learn from Mr. Mackie, who has all suspicious vessels in this port carefully watched, that the observation maintained on the *Cap Trafalgar* by the port authorities is now really efficient, and I feel sure that the Argentine Government are sincerely anxious to maintain the neutrality of this country and to prevent belligerent Powers from using Argentine ports for any illegal purpose.

The Master of the French steamer *Lutétia* to whom the Chargé d'Affaires referred was Captain Raoul Dupuy-Frey, and as Norman correctly stated, the *Lutétia* had been berthed next to *Cap Trafalgar*. In a detailed note dated August 17, Dupuy-Frey was in no doubt that his neighbor was an armed cruiser in disguise. His belief was founded on three observations:

First, he had read in a local newspaper that the *Kronprinz Wilhelm* had been surprised while arming at sea in the North Atlantic. He argued that the *Cap Trafalgar* had come through the North Atlantic herself and was also German. Therefore, she had probably armed herself on the way across. It was inspired Gallic logic.

Second, and perhaps more validly, he compared the so-called "inspection" of the *Cap Trafalgar* with the similar inspection his own ship had undergone by the same authorities at the request of the German Consul. This consisted of little more than a courteous visit to the bridge with a speedy adjournment to the cool delights of the officers' wardroom, where a bottle or two had been broached.

His third point had considerable significance. He, himself,

had been forbidden to take on coal or stores at night by an officious port officer. He had noticed that no such restriction had been placed on the *Cap Trafalgar*. "It would," he speculated, "be interesting to know why."

It was now necessary for either the British Consul or the Chargé d'Affaires to concern himself with finding out how the *Cap Trafalgar* had managed to work at night. The following morning, on August 18, at the time Norman's detailed telegram to London arrived in Whitehall, they received word from the docks that the *Cap Trafalgar* had vanished.

Commandant Langerhannsz had no illusions as to the problems he faced while in Buenos Aires. He managed to cope with the brusque incivilities of many of the port officials, for he was a popular man and behind him there was an influential local German community, who very naturally, sensing the overt hostility of the Argentines and a British-inspired press campaign, decided to keep a low profile, rendering what assistance they could as discreetly as possible. The inspections by the authorities were no hazard, for it was perfectly true that the only weapons he had on board were his own pistol and a pair of shotguns that had been presented to him several years previously. He kept quiet about the shotguns but offered to hand over his pistol as evidence of good faith. He had no worries about the Argentines finding anything else for the simple reason that there was nothing for them to find.

For the first week after the outbreak of war, he had concentrated on trying to refuel his ship. Eventually after a certain amount of discreet bribery financed by the German community, he managed to load 3,500 tons of coal under the noses of the authorities. The coal was largely loaded by night, without the help of loading lights. In the same way he took on fresh water and provisions, but, so as not to alarm the authorities, he took on exactly what could be construed as his normal requirement. Understandably, they were up to the customary standards of luxury that were associated with the flagship of the line.

His first intention had been to sail on his normal date—the 10th—and head for home. However, as the refueling and provisioning delays multiplied, his sailing date was inexorably delayed. Then came a second problem. It became apparent that he would never be able to take on sufficient coal to make a high-speed dash home. Regretfully, he decided to head for the United States, hoping to take on more coal as he slipped northward along the coast of South America, sheltering if possible in neutral territorial waters.

Langerhannsz was no coward. He was a professional merchant seaman, with a responsibility to his passengers and for the safety of his ship. As a German citizen, he certainly owed a duty to his country and to his countrymen, but he was commanding a civilian ship, and he was a civilian himself. He behaved in exactly the same way as his English counterparts in command of unarmed passenger steamers.

He did not dare to declare his real destination to the authorities. Equally difficult for him was the fact that he was already heavily booked with passengers who had a variety of reasons for wanting to return to Germany. To those who were reservists or volunteers anxious to return home as soon as possible, he magnified the considerable delays to which the uncooperative Argentines were subjecting him. He recommended that they take passage on one of the steamers that the German Consul had delegated for the task. It was a different category of passenger who worried him.

For example, there was a small touring light-opera company, complete with their scenery, props, and instruments. They had been offering a refreshing diet of Mozart and Wagner to German communities along the eastern seaboard. They had little or no money or chance of survival in Argentina and, apart from their theatrical effects, hardly anything else except their tickets home. These Langerhannsz accepted as passengers, confident that they would at least be as well off in the United States as in Buenos Aires.

There were several wives and elderly dependents of Germans who had been working in Argentina. Their husbands or sons had already left home to join the German forces, and the *Cap Trafalgar* was the first choice of those left behind, simply because it was the largest and looked the safest and smartest ship in the port. The most irritating passenger was a formidable elderly gentleman called Dr. Braunholz, who arrived on board accompanied by a large crate containing two large pigs.

The doctor was an unworldly veterinary, who had recently arrived in Buenos Aires complete with his pigs and a grandiose dream of breeding from them, and with their progeny upgrading the native Argentine pigs, which, by German standards, were undersized and hardly "wurstworthy." He had fallen foul of the port health authorities and had been peremptorily assigned to the *Cap Trafalgar* to be returned from whence he came. Langerhannsz did not take kindly to the doctor, but he did realize that he would never be allowed to land his pigs in the United States, so privately he looked forward to an excellent meal in due course.

It was the doctor's habit of interfering with everything that went on that exasperated the Captain. He condemned the kitchens, which were the *Cap Trafalgar*'s greatest pride. They were, he said, badly planned, unhygienic, and deplorably kept. He found fault with almost everything: most particularly with the Winter Garden—its livestock, its design, the variety and stocking of the birds, and their diet. When he attempted to keep his pigs there, Langerhannsz exploded. The matter had been brought to his attention by his first officer, Lieutenant Feddersen.

37

Feddersen was a tall, rangy man with a considerable sense of humor. He was a member of the German Naval Reserve but had stayed with his Captain because the ship was critically short of officers and, possibly, because he felt that, if the German Admiralty ever came round to requisitioning the ship as an armed cruiser, then as a reservist he would very probably become her commanding officer. He stood silently while Langerhannsz vented his temper on the human race in general and the wretched Dr. Braunholz in particular. When the tirade ceased, Feddersen offered a solution.

Germany, he said, was now at war. Aboard ship, the Captain's word was law at any time, and during wartime it became the equivalent of holy writ. What Dr. Braunholz needed was to be kept busy, and he also needed to be instilled with a sense of duty and obligation to the Reich. He suggested that Langerhannsz go through the motions of formally requisitioning the pigs in the name of the Reich and, for good measure, formally conscripting Braunholz as a member of the ship's company. After all, they were shorthanded, and their peacetime bird keeper had been called back to Germany.

The idea appealed to the Captain. Quickly his cabin was given a naval appearance. The German flag was spread over his desk. Feddersen lent him his reserve officer's cap. A petty officer, brought into the secret, was handed one of Langerhannsz's shotguns and stationed outside the door as a sentry. Then the ship's master at arms was sent to fetch the doctor. The summons was abrupt, and moments later the perspiring veterinary stood mopping his brow in front of the seated Captain. Feddersen stood beside the desk.

Langerhannsz cleared his throat, then, picking up some papers, read through the relevant portion of the ship's articles setting out the Captain's powers and responsibilities. Then, in a stern voice, he formally announced that by virtue of the authority vested in him, as from noon Saturday, August 15,

1914, Hans Joachim Braunholz, Doctor of Veterinary Surgery, was hereby appointed as a "Naval Zoological Attendant 2nd Class" on an unpaid basis. He would, he was told, be answerable for the feeding, maintenance, and daily care of the birds and all other livestock aboard the ship. He was responsible for the cleanliness and efficient operation of the Winter Garden. He would be reaccommodated in the crews' quarters and would be expected to render a daily report as to the well-being of his charges. As an afterthought, the pigs would be housed in the open air aft of the stern winches, and should there be the slightest offensive odor, they would be removed forthwith to the ship's butcher. Lastly, he was reminded that he was now subject to the full rigor of ship's discipline and that he was not to address an officer or petty officer unless he was spoken to. Had he any questions?

Dr. Braunholz, to everyone's surprise, was delighted. He explained that it had always been his dream to serve the Reich. The only purpose of his pig-breeding venture to Argentina had been to prove that German pigs and German breeding techniques were infinitely superior to all others. He had only one question. Might he have a uniform?

He was told to wear the white tropical jacket and cap of his predecessor as bird keeper and then was dismissed before Langerhannsz and Feddersen gave the game away by laughing.

Their laughter did not last long. While they were still in the cabin, the master of arms announced a visitor: Korvette Kapitän Müller of the Imperial German Navy, fresh from New York and newly appointed as Naval Attaché to the Republic of Argentina.

Langerhannsz was unaware that he was still wearing Feddersen's cap. Being a civilian and relatively ignorant of naval etiquette, he neither offered nor acknowledged Müller's salute. Instead he just indicated with a wave of his hand that his guest should take a seat, remarked that a visitor such as Müller was an excellent excuse for some refreshment, and rang for his steward. It took Müller quite a few minutes to work out who was who and exactly what was going on. It appeared to him that the Captain of the *Cap Trafalgar* brought a somewhat surreal quality to his duties. A glass of hock speedily resolved matters, and he enjoyed the story of Doctor Braunholz's induction as much as the others. Then, opening his briefcase, he got down to business.

He announced that on behalf of the Reich he was formally requisitioning the *Cap Trafalgar* into the Imperial German Navy. Until further instructions were received, Langerhannsz would remain in command, with Feddersen as his First Lieutenant. He then specified a lengthy list of responsibilities, closing with the remark that, in an operational situation, Langerhannsz would sail the ship, but Feddersen, because of his naval training, was to fight it.

Langerhannsz gently inquired, "With what?" He explained that all reservists and quite a few additional volunteers had already left for Germany. He was considerably under strength. His stokehold was largely manned with specialists in *opera buffa* as opposed to stokers. He had barely enough coal to travel a thousand miles, and at the moment his crew was out of sight belowdecks engaged in splitting railway ties to use as fuel.

Furthermore, he had around sixty passengers on board who were most definitely of noncombatant status, ranging from children to grandmothers, and as was usual in a long-distance luxury liner, his remaining crew included a considerable number of women, cabin stewardesses, laundry workers, nurses, and so on. Much more to the point, the sentry at the door was carrying exactly 50 percent of his armament.

He went on to explain that the Argentine authorities were being far from helpful, that it was common gossip in the port that the mouth of the Río de la Plata, down which he would have to sail, was being patrolled by British cruisers. Doubtless Admiral Tirpitz, who had obviously authorized Kapitän Müller, was aware of all this.

Müller explained that the state of affairs as outlined by Langerhannsz was very far from what he had been led to believe. He told how he had come down the coast on an American collier called the *Berwind* as far as Montevideo, which stands at the mouth of the Río de la Plata. It was true, he confirmed, that the Royal Navy was present in some force, but as regards armament and the shortage of crew, he had understood that the *Cap Trafalgar* had left Hamburg with her full complement of guns hidden in the holds, that a large percentage of the crew were trained reservists, and that instructions had been radioed from Berlin that they were to stay aboard. Nevertheless, he accepted the Captain's assertions and, after making a detailed note of the number of men of serviceable age together with the fuel aboard the *Cap Trafalgar*, returned to the German Legation to send an urgent message to Berlin.

In 1914, diplomatic messages were not sent by radio. The distances and atmospheric conditions were too much for the then relatively unsophisticated equipment. Every nation depended on the international cable networks, and these mostly belonged to Great Britain. It is a historical fact that every tiny electrical charge that pulsed along the undersea cables from the American continents to Europe passed through London. By an agreement between the British Government and the cable companies, a copy of every cable, irrespective of its language, destination, or content, was sent to Naval Intelligence.

The British did not have the keys to the German ciphers, but they had acquired a considerable knowledge of the originating and destination prefixes and suffixes, so that they knew from whom a cable was sent and to whom it was addressed. They also had, over a considerable period of monitoring, gleaned one or two vitally important clues as to what a cable might be about. In the case of Captain Müller's cable, they knew it came from Buenos Aires, was addressed to the German Admiralty, was classified as urgent and most secret, and, perhaps more important, that it referred to the *Cap Trafalgar*.

These clues were established fairly quickly. As a result, a copy was sent to Admiral Oliver, then Chief of Naval Intelligence, who, in turn, passed it to a small cryptographic team he had recently recruited, with orders to spend the weekend of August 15 and 16 trying to decipher it.

Müller's cable arrived at the Kaiser's General Headquarters on Sunday morning. It was addressed to the Naval Chief of Staff, von Pohl. According to Admiral Tirpitz, it did not reach him until the following Tuesday and had been considerably emasculated. It merely stated that the *Cap Trafalgar* was short of officers and found it impossible to obtain sufficient fuel in Buenos Aires. Tirpitz cabled back that *Cap Trafalgar* was to slip down river to Montevideo, that the German authorities there were to be responsible for filling her bunkers, and that her complement of officers was to be made up from other ships in the port. Thereafter she was to remain in Montevideo until operational orders were sent out. At the time, Tirpitz was unaware that she was unarmed.

The Cunard Company's official history states that H.M. auxiliary cruiser *Carmania* was at sea, fully armed and operational, by Friday, August 14. It is a modest stretching of a tiny point. She was anchored in the Mersey awaiting Captain Grant, who, according to Captain Barr's diary, had been summoned to the Admiralty on the evening of August 12 for last-minute orders and discussions. In his absence, Barr, in order to clear dock space and at the request of the dockyard superintendent, had taken her out into the fairway, leaving a boat's crew to bring Captain Grant out to his ship.

Barr wondered what sort of mission *Carmania* was to be given. It had been strange that Grant had had to travel to London for his briefing. Usually, or at least as had happened with the other converted cruisers, the operational briefing was given by an official called the Senior Naval Officer or S.N.O., of which there was one to each port. This official—usually an admiral or a senior captain—was in constant touch with the Admiralty, and responsible for the briefing and the prompt departure of each ship.

The S.N.O. Liverpool had indeed come aboard the previous morning and handed over a bunch of Admiralty charts with the latest minefields and wartime hazards marked on them, together with a set of signal and code books. In Grant's absence Barr had signed for them. He had also signed his name for the usual packet of sealed instructions, which would be opened once the ship was well clear of land and which would allocate the *Carmania* her patrol area. Throughout the week of conversion, both Barr and Grant had continually been told that the *Carmania* was to be utilized on the North Atlantic patrol. Her duties would be to patrol up to a hundred miles off shore. She was to stop, board, and inspect, using her Marine infantry, any merchantmen not flying the British flag.*

---

* By 1914, the world's maritime nations had adopted a set of ground rules for the conduct of sea warfare. These were embodied in the Treaty of London of 1912. They were framed almost as drafted by King Henry VIII of England when he sent an expedition to Guienne in 1512. Briefly, an unarmed ship, whether neutral or not, could be halted and inspected. If it was a neutral, it was to be set free. A merchant ship belonging to an enemy and its cargo became prizes of war, while crew and passengers became hostages. The capturing ship had the right to put a "prize crew" on board, to take the prize back to their home port. If however, there were insufficient men for a prize crew, or the distance home was too great, then the prize could be sunk. Armed merchant ships were to be treated as warships, and neutral ships

There were very few other tasks that she was fitted for. Barr tried to calculate what they might be. She was far too large a target to be used in an offensive role against German warships and far too extravagant in fuel to make extended cruises. A single Atlantic crossing took 90 percent of her bunker capacity, and as she was now a warship she would be unable to obtain fuel except in England or from some European port in Allied hands. Her logical operational area was off the coasts of Britain, where her total range of 2,400 miles would allow her to cruise at 16 knots for a maximum of 150 hours or seven days. By lowering her speed, she could extend her range, but by the same yardstick the obligation to zigzag and in case of emergency to work up to a maximum speed meant a corresponding decrease.

She was almost impossible to refuel at sea. Her freeboard was far too high to be served by a collier, and she was not equipped with coaling cranes, merely light derricks. If she attempted to coal from another vessel at sea, the requirements would be a dead calm, and some thousand lifts of coal into cargo holds, from whence it would have to be manhandled down to the stokehold. A dead calm for the duration of a thousand derrick lifts, each of around five minutes, including loading, hoisting, and unloading, would take one hundred hours nonstop. Such weather conditions just did not exist in the Atlantic. On this logic, Barr convinced himself that their mission was almost certainly to be the short North Atlantic patrols, possibly, if wind and weather were in their favor, venturing up to St. John's in Newfoundland—provided the German Fleet was not in the area. With any luck, they might be allocated a spell of Mediterranean duty, which Barr's sixty-

---

carrying contraband or munitions to an enemy port were liable to confiscation. The law had been mainly insisted upon by the United States as a result of the blockade-running activities during the Civil War. A neutral ship that carried armament was in an equivocal position, and the maritime powers were and are unable to agree on her legal status.

year-old bones infinitely preferred to wintry spells on the open bridge in the North Atlantic.

The decision to move the ship into the middle of the Mersey had been a difficult one. Technically he was not in command; he was subordinate to Grant. However, he felt it was justified. The dockyard needed their berth, and the *Carmania* had a reputation as being a cow to handle in confined spaces. She had three propellers and these took a bit of getting used to. Grant, on his own admission, had been ashore for several months, and when Barr had checked him up in the Navy list, he could not but notice that the *Carmania* was far and away the largest vessel Grant had ever seen service in, let alone commanded. Barr consoled himself that, if matters had been the other way around, the Cunard Company would never have allowed a total stranger to ease the *Carmania* out of the dock into the tidal river, execute the difficult turn, almost in her own length, and berth her in the main channel. All the same, despite his eagerness to know the full details of their sailing orders, he was markedly apprehensive about Captain Grant's return.

It had been a difficult decision to make when he had been offered the post as adviser to the man, almost fifteen years younger than himself, who was going to take his place. It had not been the offer of temporary rank in the Royal Naval Reserve that had tipped the scale. It was just that deep down he could not bear to be parted from his ship. He knew that, at his age, once he went ashore he would probably be there for life. He had responded to the invitation Grant had brought, saying simply, "I'm *your* man, Captain Grant." "Thank you, Commander," Grant had replied and then, installing himself in Barr's day cabin, had requested the *Carmania*'s ship's papers, engine-room reports, crew lists, and copies of all the officers' personal records. Thereafter he kept to himself for the remainder of the day.

Barr had his personal gear taken out of his adjoining night cabin, and after a moment's thought as to where to billet himself, had them installed in the rather more opulent suite reserved for directors of Cunard or very important passengers. As a concession to the efficiency of the ship, he gave orders for a set of voice pipes to be installed from the suite to the bridge and down to the engine room. Then, realizing that his wife and family were expecting him at home, he prepared to go ashore. Slipping his shaving kit into an overnight bag, and, from force of habit, collecting his laundry bag, he made his way to the gangway. A marine sentry was already on duty, rifle at the ready.

"Shore pass, sir," the sentry inquired. Barr cursed himself and went back to Grant, knocked at the door, and waited. He knocked louder, then opened the door.

Grant seemed surprised to see him. Shore passes he reminded Barr were issued by the first officer, who as it happened was ashore himself. He was sorry, but each man had his allotted responsibility, and he did not wish to start off by making exceptions for anyone. Barr dug his toes in. He informed Grant that he was going ashore to make his voyage report to the board of Cunard and hand over his accounts for the voyage, and, if Captain Grant did not wish him to do so, then perhaps he would pick up the telephone and inform Cunard, whose headquarters towered over the docks. Grant thawed out sufficiently to sign a pass, leaving the time of return blank.

After completing his business at Cunard, Barr took a hansom cab to his home and briefly explained to his family why he would not be joining them for the Scottish holiday. His wife approved his decision, but could not understand how anyone could sleep aboard the *Carmania* while the ship-wrights gutted her passenger accommodations, welded on her new armor plate, and installed her magazines and armament. She promptly sent a note to Captain Grant, offering him the spare room in the house while, and she phrased it with care, *"your* ship is undergoing conversion work." A civil reply came back by return, declining the invitation, regretting that he felt a captain should stay with his ship, adding that he had much to discuss with Captain Barr at Captain Barr's earliest convenience.

The relationship between the two men remained at a wary arms' length for most of that hectic week of conversion. Barr came home each evening, rejoining the ship at 6 A.M. each morning. As far as possible he tried to keep out of the way. Most of the permanent crew and officers who were remaining aboard were reservists; others were volunteers. All naturally looked to Barr as the Captain. They found the transition difficult to remember. Barr himself wrote afterward that "a Captain's job is that of a man apart. The fact that Captain Grant now played that part relieved me not a whit. There can only be one Captain, and *he was* the Captain. It was such a short time since I had been that to many I was still, and so to them, I was still a man apart. So it came about that both of us, Grant and I, who were men who loved their fellow men, were perhaps a little lonely. One cannot quarrel with this. Grant sent for me when he wished to see me. Received me pleasantly—if I had anything to report. I had told him I was his man and I lived up to it throughout."

On the evening of Wednesday, August 12, Grant had announced that he had to take the night train to London for consultations at the Admiralty. Under naval regulations command would devolve onto the first officer, Lieutenant Commander Lockyer, who had arrived with Grant and who was a gunnery specialist. Grant had solved the difficult problem of protocol by calling both Lockyer and Barr together, told them of his trip, and remarked that there was still a considerable amount of work to be done before he returned and the *Carmania* was ready for sea. He suggested that Barr see to the ship, Lockyer to the installation of the armament. Now on the Saturday morning, Barr stood on the bridge, awaiting his Captain, and anxious to know what the next few days held in store.

Captain Grant came aboard at 10 A.M. After a brief look around, he asked if steam was up. On being assured that it was, he turned to Barr and, with the hint of a smile, remarked, "Will you please take her out, Commander Barr?" For the last time in his career, James Barr slowly eased the *Carmania* into the tidal stream, thence into the North Channel, over the bar of the Mersey, and into the Irish Sea.

Captain Grant had a private reason to be pleased with himself. Barr noticed the difference of mood the moment he came aboard and put it down to the fact that he was delighted to be going to sea again at last. He never guessed the reason, for during their service together Grant never told him. However, the duty records of the British Admiralty give a substantial clue. They do not record even a whisper of any special orders or a briefing for either *Carmania* or her Captain. There is however a laconic note at the head of his personal file:

Date of marriage . . . . August 13, 1914.

It is likely that Grant was only in London long enough to obtain a special license to get married. The records of Thomas F. Litler, the registrar of births, deaths, and marriages for Liverpool, show that he married Noel Grant and May Annie Vaughan, the divorced wife of Francis Vaughan, on the afternoon of August 13 at Liverpool Registry Office. While Captain Barr eased the *Carmania* into the Mersey, Captain Grant and his bride, if they had been so inclined, could have watched them from the Adelphi Hotel, where they spent their twelve-hour honeymoon.

CERTIFIED COPY OF AN ENTRY OF MARRIAGE

Given at the GENERAL REGISTER OFFICE, LONDON

Application Number 7352G

Registration District   Liverpool

19 44 . Marriage solemnized at The Register Office
in the District of Liverpool   in the County of Liverpool

No.	When married	Name and Surname	Age	Condition	Rank or profession	Residence at the time of marriage	Father's name and surname	Rank or profession of father
27	Thirteenth August 1944	Trevitt Noel Grant	45 years	Bachelor	Captain in Royal Navy	Adelphi Hotel Liverpool	John Miller Grant (deceased)	Gentleman
		May Annie Vaughan formerly Allen spinster Joan Cantardel Vaughan	35	The divorced wife of Francis	—	46 Lancaster Gate London	Edward Allen (deceased)	Gentleman

Married in the Register Office according to the _____ of the _____ by Licence by me

This marriage was solemnized between us, { Trevitt Noel Grant / May Annie Vaughan } in the presence of us, { D. Bishop / M.J. Edwards }   Thomas Little, Registrar / J.M. Smyth Supt Registrar

CERTIFIED to be a true copy of an entry in the certified copy of a Register of Marriages in the District above mentioned.

Given at the GENERAL REGISTER OFFICE, LONDON, under the Seal of the said Office, the   13ᵗ   day of   August   19 76 .

MB 100701

Form A513 (S.349704) Dd. 151931 40M 10/74 Hw.

ꙮ 3 ꙮ

Captain Grant's first concern was to get to know his command. The *Carmania* now carried a crew of 420. The engineer, officers, and every one of the 137 greasers, firemen, and trimmers were all members of the regular crew, who had volunteered *en bloc* for active service. Each man had been given a special six-month contract with the Naval Reserve. The medical team, the radio operators, the steward, and most of the skilled artisans aboard were also Cunard men. The imported naval contingent, apart from the 38 Royal Marines, totaled 62, and they were all experienced seamen, being drawn from members of the Scottish herring fleets, who had joined the reserve for a little extra money during peacetime.

As the Cunard official history remarked, they were "Scottish fishermen of the best type." Quite what this means is difficult to define at a remove of sixty years, but one point is obvious, if they were Scottish fishermen, then they were basically sailing men, unaccustomed to the use of sophisticated machinery, the overwhelming size of the vessel, or the rigorous discipline characteristic of the Royal Navy. They would have been dour, rugged individualists, brawny and weatherwise, brought up to sail by the feel of the wind on their cheeks and the motion of their craft in a seaway. They would have had a nose for the presence of fish or the bouquet of a dram of whisky, and a total disinclination to scrub decks, polish brass, or wear a uniform. Universally, they would have had a withering contempt for any vessel powered by steam.

They were accustomed—as was Captain Barr—to light a ruminative pipe when they felt like it, to chew a wad of tobacco while they worked, and would have been none too choosy where they spat their plug as long as it was to windward. Many would have been Gaelic-speaking, and those who spoke English would have had the leisurely soft brogue of the Scottish highlands. To command such men requires a personal and oblique approach. An order has to be given politely, more as a suggestion, with the merest undertone of authority.

In the Royal Navy most orders were given by whistle, or, to be precise, by the bosun's pipe. The Navy expected commands to be carried out on the double and clamped down on anyone who thought differently. For the first few days at sea, the morning disciplinary proceedings known as "captain's orders," when defaulters were paraded for punishment, were a sorry procession of recalcitrant Scotsmen, excusing themselves for not instantly obeying what they described as "yon silly wee man with his silly wee whistle."

It is to Grant's credit that he quickly abandoned, insofar as the members of the crew were concerned, his lifelong habit of rigid adherence to the regulations. However, to compensate, he took a very different line with his officers, who, with the exception of Lieutenant Commander Lockyer, his first lieutenant, and four young midshipmen on their first voyage, were all Cunarders. Most of them were members of the *Carmania*'s regular crew. To them, Grant presented an aloof almost remote presence, withering in his criticisms, exacting in his standards, and seemingly oblivious of the extraordinary conflict of loyalties that each one of them had to overcome in his own way.

For the last two years they had all regarded Captain Barr as their chief. The Cunard Company operated on a basis of rigid discipline on duty and easy camaraderie off duty. It was only too easy to make a slip and fall foul of Grant, who appeared to be on duty twenty-four hours a day. It was, of course, equally difficult for Grant, perhaps more so as he was still far from well. In some way he had to make it plain to everyone that it was he and he alone who was in command. He made his move the second night at sea. Lieutenant Commander Lockyer was the officer in charge of the bridge at the time. Aft of him, several of the other officers, all Cunard men, were clustered, anxiously peering into the darkness as the *Carmania* headed out into the Atlantic, where for all they knew the enemy might lie in wait. Toward midnight, Captain Barr joined them. From force of habit he reached into his pocket, rummaged for his pipe, and after stuffing it to his satisfaction struck his match.

Grant, who had silently joined the group, immediately snapped an order. "Put that bloody light out—report to me in my cabin—I will not have smoking on *my* bridge." By breakfast the entire ship knew who was in command.

These were minor incidents as the *Carmania* and her cocktail of a crew shook down and began to know each other and their new work. As had been expected, their assignment was to patrol an area approximately one hundred miles square which straddled the main east-west shipping lanes to the northwest of Ireland. The southeasterly corner of the box came to within twelve miles of the coast of Donegal. This had been designated by the Admiralty as Patrol Area 18. Their task was to identify each and every vessel passing through. In the case of the slightest doubt as to the identity of any ship sighted, then they were to stop her, send over a boarding party, and inspect her papers and cargo. It was dreary work,

52

for many of the smaller vessels inward bound had left their ports of departure before hostilities had commenced and were therefore ignorant of the recently disinterred rules for identification. At the same time, the *Carmania* was to act as a scout and keep an eye open for enemy warships and submarines.

Apart from these everyday duties, there were the chores of marking up the Admiralty charts supplied to them and constant battle drill. The gunnery control gear was rigged, a dummy target thrown over the stern; the gunners then practiced until they learned to shoot reasonably straight.

The *Carmania* had been fitted with eight 4.7-inch guns. Two were mounted forward, two aft, and two amidships on each side. This gave a broadside of four, but, owing to the curvature of the hull, it was found that if she presented her stern quarter to an enemy, then both the stern guns had a clear field of fire, giving a total salvo of five guns at once.

The firing practice had the side effect of cementing the relationships among the members of the crew. The nineteen Marine gunners who manned the eight 4.7-inchers were fully employed in laying and firing. They relied on the ordinary seamen to bring up the ammunition, and the seamen in their turn were given the chance to learn how to load, aim, and fire. Grant cleverly arranged the watches so that they built around the gun crews. The gunners, who had tended to regard themselves as a race apart, were asked to assist with other shipboard watch duties, while the seamen, in exchange, assisted with the care, maintenance, and operation of the guns.

Similarly, the Marine boarding party were mixed with seamen. The Scottish fishermen were far more experienced in handling the small ship's boats in a heavy swell than were the Marine infantry. Slowly, and with increasingly good humor, the *Carmania* became a reasonably efficient auxiliary cruiser, capable of handling the relatively simple tasks to which she had been assigned.

The officers took slightly longer to settle down. The eight guns were commanded by four Cunarders, who had been in the Naval Reserve. Each had spent a fortnight each year training with the Navy, and one of them, Lieutenant Murchie, who had been the *Carmania*'s chief officer in peacetime, had actually done a gunnery course. Each officer had charge of a pair of guns and each was responsible to the regular Navy officer, Lieutenant Commander Lockyer, who stood on top of the bridge with his rangefinder and binoculars to control the fire.

Lockyer's orders were transmitted by a battery of field telephones, one phone to each pair of guns. Lines festooned the deck, leading from the bridge down to the individual gun officers on the decks. Bridge and decks were completely open to wind and weather, so even in a modest wind speech was almost unintelligible. The *Carmania* had not been designed as a warship, so the gun positions, with the exception of the pair on the foredeck, were out of Lockyer's sight.

A compromise system was devised, whereby Lockyer shouted his orders to a seaman stationed below him, who passed them to another man within earshot, and so on down the length of the ship. As the *Carmania* was over two hundred yards long, messages were garbled. When Lockyer ordered a salvo, which the Royal Navy decreed should be simultaneous, the *Carmania*'s was a staccato chorus of gunfire which rumbled from stem to stern.

A naval gunnery officer's problems are legion. One is to allow for the roll or heel of the ship. As the *Carmania* stood far higher out of the water than a warship, the effect of a heel could substantially increase or decrease the calibrated range of the guns. A roll of 10 percent off the vertical to either port or starboard added or subtracted 10 percent of their elevation or depression. If Lockyer ordered "Fire" at the start of a roll to starboard, the stern gun usually got the message as the ship settled down again on her port side. With the guns set at their maximum elevation for nine thousand yards, the combined effect was for the salvo to fall anything up to half a mile over or short of the target. Again a compromise was adopted. Crews were trained so that Lockyer would give the order to fire while she was on an even keel. Each crew would then wait until the ship had completed her roll and returned to an even keel again. By this time the orders would, or should, have reached every gun on the ship, and a reasonably simultaneous and equally ranged salvo would be fired. It was a method of fire control that had worked excellently at Trafalgar, and in the absence of the hydraulic controls available on a modern warship, it was the best solution available.

Voice control was normal in the liners of that time but added sorely to the problems of controlling a warship. It was obvious to Grant that, with the *Carmania*'s exposed bridge, in any action, not only would he be unable to hear himself speak but no one else would be able to hear him either.

He had been told that when Barr took the *Carmania* out of the conversion dock into the River Mersey he had, most unusually, directed her from the stern. He asked why. Barr explained that the stern was invisible from the bridge and, in addition, moved extra swiftly, as the *Carmania* was triple screwed. Her three propellers could be used independently. At low speed, which is when a ship is at its most unwieldy, he often used them to give the *Carmania* a quick nudge (or squirt, as he described it) in one direction or another. The trick was to play the thrust of one propeller against the rudder. He had found that she was slow to respond to her helm from the bridge wheel, as the maze of cables, gears, and pumps tended to take their time as they transmitted the wheel's instructions to the rudder.

On his own initiative, he had had a voice pipe rigged on the stern that led directly down to the "tiller flat" below the water line. This, together with a second set of engine-room controls, gave him a direct and instant contact with the ship's engine and steering gear and enabled him to gauge the *Carmania*'s docking or undocking to a nicety.

Apart from himself, he had trained his peacetime navigator, Lieutenant Battle, to operate the gear down on the tiller flat.

In fact, Barr had anticipated the control system in use today among unwieldy vessels such as oil tankers, but his motive had been very different. The Cunard Company paid a bonus to its captains if they were able to dock or undock with a minimum or, at best, complete absence of tugs. Barr had worked out his system in an effort to increase his bonuses. Grant was impressed and immediately saw the tactical advantages.

Thereafter, every time the *Carmania* went to practice battle stations, Lieutenant Battle was sent down to the tiller flat, and all bridge officers learned to maneuver the ship from the stern position, so that, in the event of the bridge or the bridge controls being damaged or shot away, she would not be helpless.

Slowly a spirit of cooperation developed, which can be attributed to a variety of causes: leadership, tradition, a common cause. There could be many answers, but there was one factor that made the *Carmania* unique in the British Navy; officers and crew fed like fighting cocks.

The *Carmania* was a luxury liner. Her food and her wines were legendary. In the rush of conversion, her refrigerated stocks and wine cellar had been left aboard. There had not been time for ordinary naval rations to be ordered. Cunard had merely loaded the same quantity of supplies as was usual. The company had always prided itself on a fast turn-around when its ships came into port, and this occasion had been no exception. While shipwrights and fitters had bustled on with the conversion, the provision vans had driven up and un-loaded their standing orders of the best Scotch salmon, sides of beef, Dover sole, eggs, cream, fresh fruit, and, to Barr's undisguised delight, grouse, victims of the first day of the hunting season.

As Barr recalled years afterward, Cunard had undoubtedly sent the Admiralty a bill for the victualing of the ship, and it would have been a crime to waste "Navy property" by letting it go bad. Luncheon and dinner in the wardroom were gargantuan. Even officers on watch could order almost what they wished and have it served upon a silver salver, carried by a white-coated steward. The ship had its own bakery, and there was fresh bread for everyone each morning. The stokers and engine-room hands each had a special allowance of four pounds of steak a day, which they preferred to grill on their shovels instead of coming up to the mess room.

The only fly in the ointment as far as the few regular Navy hands were concerned was a shortage of rum. This, however, suited the Scotsmen, who happily took their grog ration in a choice of fine malt whiskies. Winston Churchill, who had once defined naval traditions as a "mixture of rum, buggery, and the lash below decks, whilst the officers learnt to drink gin like gentlemen," would have been agreeably surprised.

Shortly after an excellent dinner on the evening of Wednesday, August 19, the duty signalman brought a coded message into the wardroom. Grant invited Barr to his cabin to help him decode it. It was short and gave no explanation. It said bluntly, "Leave patrol station immediately. Proceed Bermuda soonest. Advise estimated time of arrival."

The exchange of cables between Buenos Aires, Berlin, and Montevideo had fascinated the British Admiralty. They rightly concluded that the *Cap Trafalgar* was going to try to break for the open sea. This was confirmed when a message arrived from the British Consulate in Buenos Aires stating that the *Cap Trafalgar* had slipped out on the night of the 17th with as far as they could estimate some 3,500 tons of coal aboard and a quantity of timber, which they believed was to be used for gun mountings.

Montevideo is a short five-hour down-river passage from Buenos Aires. When, by the evening of Tuesday, August 18, the *Cap Trafalgar* had neither been sighted in nor outside the harbor, the Admiralty concluded that she had slipped past in the night and escaped into the Atlantic. With her estimated coal stocks, she was, they reckoned, either making for the United States or possibly making a dash for German Southwest Africa. On this latter assumption, the blockading cruisers off the Plata estuary were ordered to head for Southwest Africa in an attempt to cut her off.

The truth of the matter was the opposite. The *Cap Trafalgar* did not leave Buenos Aires on the 17th, but merely moved further out to another berth in the roads outside the main harbor. In this way she hoped to slip away without being seen. What had fooled the consulate was that she had obtained *clearance to sail* on the 17th from the port authorities, and on the evidence of this clearance her departure had been reported to London.

Korvette Kapitän Müller came out to meet Langerhannsz on Tuesday afternoon. He brought with him instructions to proceed as soon as possible to Montevideo, where it was hoped coal would be waiting. Equally he expected there would be some extra officers. Müller suggested that he come himself as a passenger. The *Cap Trafalgar* slipped her moorings during the evening and arrived a few miles off Montevideo the following morning, Wednesday, August 19.

The weather was bad, a short ugly swell, with squalls of rain and mist. It was no weather in which to coal, so

Langerhannsz hovered off the coast, riding out the storm, and keeping a wary radio watch for the blockading British cruisers. It was not until dawn on Saturday, August 22, that he managed to enter the harbor, and as soon as his papers had been cleared, he started to load the coal Admiral Tirpitz had ordered for him.

By this time, the *Good Hope* was well on her way to Africa, and the *Carmania* had been hauled in off the North Atlantic patrol and was making full speed to Bermuda, where the Admiralty wished her to replace the *Good Hope* temporarily. Unaware of the reception being planned for him, Langerhannsz opened his hatches and commenced to coal.

Captain Müller went ashore to the legation in Montevideo. He quickly explained that Langerhannsz had neither armament nor ammunition and reported the presence of the various refugee passengers and the shortage of officers. It was a time for immediate decision, and Müller prompted the somewhat reluctant German Minister to help him. The fact that it was a Saturday was both a help and a hindrance. The various authorities who could hinder them were observing their weekend, but finding anyone to help was also a problem. Without authority, Müller had himself rowed out to the German steamer *Camerones,* which had several naval officers on her crew list. He ordered First Officer Lange and Third Officer Schreiner to pack their gear and join the *Cap Trafalgar* at once. Taking them with him, he then returned to the *Cap Trafalgar.*

When they arrived he found a message from Berlin ordering the *Cap Trafalgar* to report immediately to Trinidad Island. All the passengers and female crew were transferred to other German steamers in the port; the men in the opera company and Dr. Braunholz opted to stay. Langerhannsz then called the crew together. None of them were liable for active service; those who had been had left the ship in Buenos Aires. He asked for volunteers, saying that they were to assume an operational role, not mentioning their destination. No one refused to sail. Langerhannsz saw little point in cluttering his ship up with pastry cooks and surplus kitchen staff or, for that matter, with the cabin stewards, who were all well past military age. His yardstick was that if a man was fit enough to take his turn as a stoker then he would keep him. Privately he considered the entire adventure ridiculous, and it was only his pride and an inborn politeness that kept him from saying so. He did, however, confide his feeling to Lieutenant Feddersen.

The *Cap Trafalgar* had barely disembarked those who were not sailing when a party of officials from the Uruguayan Government arrived. Fortunately Langerhannsz knew one of them well. He gave his word of honor that he was not armed and the official agreed not to search his ship. Others poked around for an hour or so, accepted a drink, and then departed, granting him clearance for Togoland via Las Palmas. He had a suspicion that this information would be in London fairly quickly. He was not mistaken.

TELEGRAM TO FOREIGN OFFICE, LONDON

SECRET   115 Treaty 7

Following facts regards German Mail Steamer

Cap Trafalgar.

August 17 following telegram received from Consul General Buenos Aires:

"German Mail Steamer *Cap Trafalgar* sailed at 5 P.M. with large quantity of timber baulks which in opinion of naval officer can only be used for gun mountings."

August 18 following telegram received Buenos Aires:

"French ship *Lutétia* to sail today with many French reserves on board, urgent desire knowledge if *Cap Trafalgar* which has taken on 3000 tons of coal is at Monte Video and whether danger threatening."

On 21 following telegram received from Buenos Aires:

"Informed that *Cap Trafalgar* which took 3500 tons of coal here is taking more at Monte Video. Admiralty notified."

Information received from English ship that *Cap Trafalgar* had quantity of timber on deck.

Authority here responsible for observance rules neutrality is the Department of War and Marine. Principal official Marine service bears familiar name of Taylor—Captain Taylor. Old friend this Legation, sentiments are entirely with the English, bears a high character.

Inspection of ships carried out under direction Captain of the Port. Bears familiar name "Lyons." Colonel Lyons a prudent, reserved, obstinate man, high character. Sympathies hard to discover, always thoroughly friendly, obstinacy occasionally troublesome.

Spoken separately, Lyons and Taylor both give identical information:

Taylor himself went aboard, being friend Captain of the ship, did not make inspection.

Minute inspection made by naval architect of government, who reported by Captain Taylor to be above suspicion. Examined holds: measured coal bunkers. Holds completely empty. Neither arms, ammunition, nor timber. Coal bunkers capacity is 4000 tons.

Took in 1600 tons, did not quite fill bunkers.

Declared herself merchant ship, bound Europe via Las Palmas.

Authorities considered under circumstances view long dangerous journey, amount not excessive.

No reason doubt accuracy of information given. Do not doubt it.

When war broke out government taken panic lest country exposed coal famine. Great difficulty stopping regulations which would [have] paralysed British shipping. On strength your telegrams detailing amounts coal already en route or to be dispatched.

President induced to refuse sanction to proposed regulations, agreed give all merchant ships quantity required to fill bunkers. This rule perfectly satisfactory our shipping, naturally applied to *Cap Trafalgar.*

Where *Cap Trafalgar* going, what she proposes to do remains a mystery. Suggested she may be trying get United States to register as American ship. Taylor believes going Africa to transport troops.

A. Mitchell-Jones

The *Cap Trafalgar* slipped her moorings at midnight August 22 exactly eighteen hours after she had arrived. Without lights she drifted slowly out on the ebb tide and into the Plata estuary. Although she had steam up, Langerhannsz was content to let the strong current carry him gently and silently out to sea. He remained on the bridge, slipping occasionally into the radio cabin, where the operator lent him a pair of headphones so that he could listen in to whatever radio traffic there was.

Far and away the loudest was the radio of the cruiser *Glasgow,* which, from the strength of the message, he judged to be about thirty miles away. At 3 A.M. he called down for full steam. Setting the *Cap Trafalgar* on a course of due east, he headed for the open sea.

He spent the remainder of the night formulating a plan of campaign. Trinidad lay roughly 1,750 miles northeast of Montevideo. He planned to put the South American coast as far behind him as possible, for he reckoned that it would be the coast that the British would be patroling. He calculated that if he steamed eastward until he reached longitude 29° 30′ west, he could turn northward and close on Trinidad from the south, which would be the last direction anyone would expect him to come from. Also, and until the last few hours of steaming, his cover story that he was heading for Las Palmas would make sense since it would agree with his course.

The second problem was more difficult. The *Cap Trafalgar* was a brand-new ship and unlikely to have her silhouette in any naval or marine reference book. If he should be sighted at a distance, his three great funnels, towering like beckoning fingers, would send every ship's captain racing to his reference book. There were no other three-funneled passenger steamers working the South American coast. His silhouette would be more like that of one of the larger German or English cruisers, any of which could blast him out of the water at a range of several miles. He had no idea what German warships were in the area. There had been reports that the *Dresden* was nearby, but he calculated that no cruiser, British or German, would come close enough to make a positive identification. His first priority was to disguise the ship.

Fortunately the aft of his three funnels was not connected to the boiler room. It served as a forced-draught ventilator to the passenger decks and the galleys, and the exhaust from the generator system. He calculated that he could dismantle it, rig trunking to clear the generator fumes, and achieve a two-funnel profile. With that achieved, the problem remained: which passenger ship should he resemble, and how many two-funneled twenty-thousand tonners were there on the high seas? The answer was, Not too many. His mind focused on the ports he had been in. Who had been in Vigo, Rio, Hamburg, Southampton whose identity he could easily borrow and safely get away with, albeit at long range? It must be a simple question of changing his paintwork, perhaps knocking up some dummy superstructure out of canvas. Seizing the voice pipe, he routed Feddersen out of his bunk.

Langerhannsz posed an oblique question. "If the lookouts reported a twin-funneled twenty-thousand-ton passenger steamer on the horizon, who could it be?"

"Ours, or theirs?" asked Feddersen.

"Theirs."

"Either a Cunarder or Union Castle, I suppose. Let's see, there's the *Carpathia,* the *Caronia,* the *Old Catalonia,* the *Carmania.* . . ."

The last name struck a chord in Langerhannsz's mind. Korvette Kapitän Müller had remarked that he had crossed to New York in the *Carmania* only a month previously. He had been interested as, like the *Cap Trafalgar,* she was driven by turbines and fitted with triple screws. Her Captain had dispensed with tugs both in the Mersey and on entering the Hudson River in New York. He had made the comparison quite idly, as Langerhannsz docked the *Cap Trafalgar* the same way in Montevideo in order to attract as little attention as possible. At the time, Langerhannsz had merely remarked that in shallow waters like the Plata estuary the extra maneuverability was a great asset. Now that he had the name in his mind, he realized that there was some other context in which he had heard or read about the *Carmania.* Quite deliberately he began to reconstruct his conversations over the last few days.

Müller had mentioned the ship—Müller—that scene in the cabin when he arrived on board, just after the joke on that dreary bore Braunholz. That was it, Braunholz had dared to compare the *Cap Trafalgar*'s kitchens with the *Carmania*'s. Within minutes, a fearful Braunholz was standing rigidly to attention in front of his Captain. It was explained to him that he had mentioned the *Carmania* while they were in Buenos Aires. What did he know about her? Braunholz began to bluster. He had been talking out of turn. The *Carmania* was a lousy ship. The cockroaches in her kitchen were the largest on the Atlantic run. The food had been appalling, the bridge games dishonest, and also it had been most embarrassing, there had been the problem of his qualifications at the time of the accident. Langerhannsz let him ramble on. Stripped of hyperbole, Braunholz's story was simple. He had shipped as a passenger aboard the *Carmania* in October, 1913. In continental style he had quite properly given his title as Doctor. He had found out that, while the English passengers regarded a doctor of medicine as worthy of conversation, in their eyes a veterinary was only one rank higher than a groom or a hunt servant. Realizing this, he had kept quiet and allowed his fellow passengers to assume he was a doctor of medicine.

In mid-Atlantic an emigrant ship called the *Volturno*, bound for Nova Scotia from Rotterdam with some seven hundred Eastern European emigrants aboard, had caught fire after a series of explosions. The *Carmania* had answered the SOS and been the first vessel to arrive on the scene. She had rescued several hundred from the burning wreck. Many were injured, and because he held the title of Doctor and spoke German, he had been called in to assist the *Carmania*'s medical staff. It had been impossible to refuse. A burnt or broken limb was rather easier to treat on a human than it was, for example, on a racehorse.

The upshot had been that the *Carmania*'s medical team, after thanking him for his assistance, had asked him where he had trained. When they realized he was a veterinary, their attitude had cooled. As the passengers heard the truth, he finished the voyage as a social outcast instead of as a hero. It had been most unjust.

Langerhannsz interrupted him. He asked him to describe the *Carmania*. Could he remember what she looked like? Could he sketch her profile? Braunholz exceeded his expectations. He took out his wallet and produced a faded clipping with photographs of the ship, her master, Captain Barr, and an artist's impression of the rescue. One glance was enough. By tonight, Langerhannsz told Feddersen, this ship must look like the *Carmania*.

ꙩ4꙯

The removal of the aft funnel was the first problem. It was made of 5/16-inch mild steel plate and towered forty feet above the boat deck. Although it had been built as detachable, it would normally have been installed or removed by a shipyard crane. At the base it was bolted down with a series of heavy castellated bolts. Additional stability came from eight steel straining cables grouped around it, secured to a collar that banded the funnel about a foot below the rim. A permanent steel inspection ladder was fixed to the port side, and on the starboard was a small inspection hatch three feet high and twenty inches wide.

Inside was a maze of venting pipes that could easily be run elsewhere. The difficulty was that it also contained a massive water condenser, which operated on the same principle as a car radiator. Excess steam from the engine room was passed into it under pressure; there it was cooled back to water, which flowed back to the tanks below deck. The question was, what would happen if the condenser was removed? Would it affect the ship's performance?

Although the *Cap Trafalgar* had had full sea trials, a great deal had yet to be learned about her. Langerhannsz and his engineering officers rooted among the engineering manuals and pipe diagrams to discover the answer. They concluded that the effect would be minimal.

The three propellers were each controlled by separate engines. Those on either side were driven by high-speed turbines, the central one by a conventional reciprocal steam engine. The condenser served only the central engine, and it was calculated that if it was removed then speed would be reduced to a maximum of sixteen knots as opposed to her designed maximum of eighteen. In order to be on the safe side, Langerhannsz decided to cut out two of the four boilers serving the central engine. This would also save coal. As insurance, he ordered that the two idle boilers be quickly refired should there be an emergency. With that agreed, work proceeded on removing the funnel itself.

As the ship was still making full speed, a novel method of dismantling was worked out. The castellated bolts were left in place, as was the collar around the top. A cradle was rigged, and a lengthy process of oxyacetylene cutting began. The cuts were made vertically down from the collar to the base. They were approximately one foot apart, so that toward evening if the collar had been removed the funnel would have opened like a flower or a peeled banana. In all, there were twenty-six of the vertical cuts, leaving twenty-seven strips of steel, each one a foot wide and forty feet high, each still bolted to the deck and still held by the collar. The lower end was then eased outward by hand, the top supported by a cable running through a pulley fixed to the collar. In this way nineteen strips were removed, leaving only the eight to which the straining cables were connected.

At this stage, the ducting pipes and the condenser were relocated to a position immediately to the rear of the central funnel. When this was completed, all that remained was to bring down the remaining eight strips and the collar.

A wire was led from the deck to the collar of the central funnel, passed through a pulley, and then secured around the eight strips so that it formed a primitive slipknot. This could be controlled from the deck. The aft collar was then unbolted and allowed to slip down to the deck. Each strip, now held only by the slip wire, the base bolts, and its individual straining cable, was unbolted at the base and eased down, the slipknot being tightened as each was removed.

It was not perhaps the most efficient method of dismantling many tons of sheet steel while rolling and pitching at full speed in a choppy sea, but it worked. The only injuries were innumerable bruises and pinched fingers. Langerhannsz was pitifully short of hands, and everyone had something to do.

While the aft funnel was being dismantled, the remaining two were repainted in the Cunard colors of red with a black top. At the same time, the lifeboats, which on the *Cap Trafalgar* were normally black with white topping, were painted white overall to match Cunard practice.

Langerhannsz's other major problem was to remodel his superstructure so that at a distance it bore a superficial resemblance to that of the *Carmania*. The trouble was that he had only Braunholz's crumpled press clipping to go by. As far as he could see, the *Carmania*'s navigation bridge stretched the width of the ship, with a chart house sitting squarely at the back of it. His own, perched like a matchbox on top of the main saloon, was little more than a railed-in area about a quarter the width of the ship.

The main saloon was cleared of furniture. On the floor a framework of light timber was made which, when erected, could be bolted onto either side of the existing navigation bridge. Over the frame, Langerhannsz decided to stretch canvas, and then paint the complete assembly. He delegated the job to the stage manager of the touring opera company.

It was an inspired decision. It appeared that among their baggage and props they had numerous backdrops. Furthermore, with two of the boilers closed down, the entire company could work on the job, all of them only too delighted to escape from the stokeholds. Singers, musicians, and actors set to with a will. As they worked someone began to strum on the saloon piano. Another started singing, and within minutes chorus after chorus began to ring through the ship. The refrains were quickly taken up by those painting the lifeboats on the boat deck outside the saloon windows. Soon, even those who could not sing joined in, feet tapped, paint brushes flew back and forth in time to the music. The *Cap Trafalgar*, visibly changing her appearance with every mile covered, throbbed westward in a panoply of song.

The dummy bridge was fitted during the afternoon of Wednesday, August 26. Once it was in place, the painters immediately set to work to blend it with the permanent superstructure. From the outside, it looked a passable job. Langerhannsz went up to the bows and found it difficult to spot where the steel work stopped and the canvas took over. From the inside of the bridge, a different picture was presented. The dummy wings had been cut from the backdrops: to his port side Langerhannsz had a jumbled view of an Italian street scene from the *Marriage of Figaro*, while to starboard, he looked on the idyllically lush greenery of a woodland glade.

The remaining problems were minor. The broad expanse of glass flanking the Winter Garden was covered over with white paint, leaving clear patches to simulate normal portholes. A canvas and timber screen was erected over the deck rails in order to give the hull a higher appearance and to screen the activities of those on deck. The boats were fully provisioned and the red ensign of Great Britain and an improvised copy of the Cunard house flag were stitched together, rolled up, and fixed to the base of the flag staffs ready to hoist in emergency. Langerhannsz made one exception to the disguise. He refused either to paint out or cover up the ship's name, which was painted prominently on bow and stern. It was not that this would have been too difficult; he just felt in his bones that it would be unlucky.

His plan was to use his speed to try to evade search or capture. The purpose of the disguise was to delay any inspection by a British warship, and more importantly, to fool any English or Allied merchant ship that came into view, which would almost certainly be bound to report his presence. With his two-funneled profile he could be one of a number of American, Italian, or Allied ships, and his Cunard colors, if anyone came near enough to note them, would throw further doubt and confusion over his true identity. Cunard had numerous ships and they were, he reasoned, spread all over the Atlantic.

Toward midnight on August 26, the *Cap Trafalgar* reached the longitude of 29° 30′ west. With considerable relief, Langerhannsz reduced to half speed, and brought his ship around to a northerly heading. Then he began the approach toward Trinidad Island, which lay some 450 miles ahead. Somewhere between the *Cap Trafalgar* and the island would be units of the German Navy, which, he had been told, would be waiting for him.

Captain Julius Wirth was still anxiously patrolling the island. The *Eber* had been cleaned up, painted warship gray by courtesy of the *Dresden,* and now presented a respectable, if not very ferocious, appearance. Since the *Dresden* had left, he had begun to feel in an alarmingly exposed position. The anchorage by the southwest corner of the island was full of little colliers, which he had to go out and identify as they approached and then guard while they unloaded. In the absence of any other orders, he also had to decide what to do with their coal. Did he keep them waiting there until the warships they were meant to rebunker arrived, or did he try to get their coal ashore? It was a difficult decision. He decided to keep them loaded and anchored at the island until coal was needed, but other cargo he landed ashore.

These small ships kept him busy. In his first week he coped with the *Berwind,* the *Pontos,* the *Santa Isabel,* and the *Eleonore Wouvermans.* The latter presented him with a minor problem. She carried, besides a full complement of coal, 350 barrels of lighting oil, hundreds of crates of food, ammunition, and, to his consternation, 40 bullocks. These he turned loose on the island. It was no easy task, as there was neither jetty nor crane available, and each bullock had to be lowered into the water and cajoled into swimming ashore. When he added these to the *Steiemark*'s pigs and chickens, he began to see himself sitting out the war as a farmer. Running a refueling depot did not suit Wirth's character, neither did he relish the responsibility of trying to install a sense of naval discipline into his flock. His major trial had been with the cargo ship *Berwind,* which arrived shortly after his rendezvous with the *Dresden.*

The *Berwind* was American owned and registered. Formerly she had been the English tramp steamer *City of Boston,* but she had been purchased by the Puerto Rican Steamship Company and her name and registry changed. The directors of this company obviously had strong German connections and sympathies and had willingly put their acquisition at the disposal of the German Naval Attaché in Washington. The identities of her owners were discreetly veiled, but it is likely that she was officered almost entirely by German residents in the United States who were members of the Naval Reserve. It is probable, but at this remove impossible to confirm, that the *Berwind* and her owners were entirely financed by the German Admiralty.

She had left New York harbor on August 5, 1914, with a

cargo of coal, provisions, and, according to an affidavit sworn on November 18, 1914, by three members of her crew before the United States Commissioner of Shipping, a considerable quantity of ammunition. She had given her destination as Buenos Aires.

The affidavit, however, tells a rather different story, and explains why, when she eventually did arrive in Argentina, her holds were empty. It was sworn to by three Spaniards: José Ríos, Manuel Sánchez, and José Díaz. All had signed on as firemen aboard her on August 3.

They claim that the first thing they noticed was that she appeared to carry a considerable number of cabin boys, stewards, and cooks. As soon as the three-mile limit was reached, these men "suddenly put away their simple garb and humility and blossomed out as officers of the German Navy."

Full naval discipline was imposed upon them, and, though the American flag was kept flying, the *Berwind* took a roundabout passage to Buenos Aires. On August 9 she rendezvoused with the German cruiser *Karlsruhe* off the West Indies, transferring the disguised officers and fresh supplies. From there she sailed down to Montevideo, where she put Korvette Kapitän Müller ashore. Stopping only to take on coal and water, she then set course for Trinidad Island, where she arrived on August 16.

She immediately began to resupply the *Dresden*. In their affidavit and in a statement to the New York *Herald* published November 19, 1914, the three Spaniards confused the *Dresden* with the *Cap Trafalgar*. At this time, the *Cap Trafalgar* was still in Buenos Aires. In order to get coal aboard, a cable was rigged between the two ships; buckets were loaded and then winched up along the cable. It was dirty, breathless work, and six members of the crew, all Spaniards, refused to do it. They protested that they had been hired to stoke the boilers, not load or unload cargo, particularly contraband to a warship.

⸱❧

The master of the *Berwind* threatened them with his revolver. Then, so they swore, they were overpowered, put in double irons, and thrown into the coal bunkers above the boilers. One man who continued to make trouble claims that he was strung up by his thumbs. The men in the bunkers, overcome by the heat and dust, begged for water. They were taken out and placed in the ship's refrigerated room. After a few hours of this, their spirits broke, and they agreed to resume transferring coal.

As they had missed two days' work during the controversy, they were fined two days' pay, and it was this stoppage that had led them to file a complaint through the Seamen's Legal Aid Society when they eventually returned to New York three months later. If it had not been for their complaint, we would know even less about exactly what happened at Trinidad.

Captain Wirth's problem was what to do with the *Berwind*. He realized that as soon as she reached the mainland again the Spanish seamen would start talking. They would either have to be kept on the island after the *Berwind* sailed or they could have an "accident." Neither course appealed to Wirth, and it was obvious to him that either alternative would bring queries from the authorities. The short-term answer was to keep the *Berwind* with him as a store ship, until they had no further use for the island as a depot or rendezvous.

The cause of the whole problem was the hastiness of the improvised arrangements made by the German naval authorities at the outbreak of war. The mistake of using neutral seamen and then antagonizing them deprived Wirth of an invaluable transport and added to his already considerable responsibilities.

Wirth had been asked to observe radio silence. Through his own set he could hear the British, and from the strength of their signals he could approximate how far away they were. He reasoned that, as the British would also be listening for

German signals, if he wished to transmit he must plan a trick. He was anxious to send some messages and decided to use the *Berwind* as a floating signal station. He gave her master a set of messages already in code, together with the *Eber*'s call sign. On August 20, he ordered her to sail due west some five hundred miles and transmit his messages to the German consulate at Rio marked for onward transmission to Berlin. One of them read: "When may I expect armed cruiser to support my operation?"

The *Berwind,* leaving the six Spaniards in charge of the bullocks, sailed immediately to a point some sixty miles off Rio. Her American registration and flag ensured that she was not molested. On the evening of August 22, Wirth's messages went out. The British cruisers picked up the transmission and added another pin to their "plot" of suspected German ships. The cable to Berlin was in turn intercepted by the British Admiralty. As they tried to put the pieces of the jigsaw together, they came to a totally logical conclusion, which Wirth had not anticipated.

They shared the belief of the blockading cruisers that there was another German warship off Rio. More important, they identified the *Eber*'s call sign. The *Eber* they believed to be operating off the African coast. This confirmed their belief that Germany was planning something fairly sinister either on the trade route from Cape Town or in West Africa itself. To counter these two threats meant a further dilution of the squadron covering the South Atlantic.

As ships were drawn south from the West Indies squadron to investigate and hopefully counterbalance the signs of German intrusion, the squadron itself had to be kept up to strength. The *Carmania,* now approaching the harbor in Bermuda, was earmarked to sail a further thousand miles south and join them as soon as she had coaled and drawn the requisite supplies for operating in tropical waters.

Grant and Barr were in urgent conference aboard the *Carmania*. The following morning they were due to enter Bermuda, which was a port that on paper was closed to them because of the twin hazards of the *Carmania*'s length and draft. The approaches were narrow and shallow. They allowed just twelve feet below the keel. It was going to demand superb navigation and ship handling to maneuver her through the tortuous maze of channels to the coaling station.

Fortunately, Grant had served in Bermuda some years previously and had been the pilot's examiner for the port. This knowledge, combined with Barr's ability to spin the *Carmania* around in confined spaces, gave them a reasonable chance of making it. Both preferred not to think what would happen if they went aground in the channel. They would block it until the *Carmania* fell to pieces, with goodness knows what consequences to the Navy's coaling station, which would then be sealed inside. The following morning, working in harmony they inched their way through, stirring up the mud beneath their keel so that it bubbled all around them, but by a combination of luck and skill avoiding touching bottom. However, they drew too much to come alongside the coaling wharf, so coal and provisions had to be brought out to them in lighters.

It had been one problem to get into the port with bunkers two-thirds empty. It was going to be far harder to rebunker and get out again with a deeper draft.

It took six days to coal the *Carmania*, and then she was able to take just over half her capacity. The Bermuda channel gave a minimum clearance of 32 feet and it was Barr's responsibility to so trim the ship that at no point from stem to stern did she draw more than 31 feet 6 inches.

The *Carmania* was awash with coal. Normally she took it in through her coaling ports, which were let into her sides. This, however, was beyond the capabilities of the lighters, so each load had to be winched aboard by the cargo derricks, then dumped on the deck, then shoveled by hand down to the bunkers. The combination of the August sun, coal dust, and humidity was not only acutely uncomfortable, but a dangerous fire hazard as well. Coal dust, if trapped in confined spaces, becomes highly volatile and will explode if given the opportunity. It called for a rigorous nonsmoking routine and close supervision to keep the boilers damped down.

Grant, who knew the port well, complained that the dust was affecting his "asthma" and spent much of his time ashore. The first officer, Lieutenant Commander Lockyer, also began to feel the strain of the heat and was content to leave the day-to-day running of the ship in Barr's hands. This suited Barr, for he spent most of the time in consultation with the engineering officers, calculating the trim of the ship, pumping water from tank to tank to keep her level. He reasoned that with both regular naval officers out of commission, if the *Carmania* did draw an inch too much on the way out of Bermuda, then he and he alone would be to blame. It was a challenge that appealed to him, though he began to wonder how long the officers would hold together if the current cruise went on for too long.

Grant was obviously not well. Throughout the voyage, so far, he had spent long periods alone in his cabin. He pecked at his food, and his hacking cough could be heard at all hours. Barr had no doubt that Grant was a perfectionist and a thoroughly capable officer. He was obviously a first-class navigator and pilot but, Barr felt, was far too frail for a protracted operational mission. Lockyer was another problem. He was certainly regular Navy, but Barr had been shattered to find that he was nearing seventy. He had retired in 1909 and secured a part-time position at the naval gunnery school at Portsmouth in order to eke out his pension. In the haste of mobilization, he too had slipped back onto full pay. There was no doubt that he was first class with his guns, but he had already been excused the more onerous watchkeeping duties. This had resulted in an extra workload falling onto the remaining officers.

Barr himself did not stand watches, but Grant had insisted that during daylight at sea one or the other of them must be on the bridge at all times. Grant also insisted that at night he and Barr take turns sleeping in the chart house behind the bridge. This was no hardship, but it deprived the watch officers of anywhere to come in and shelter from the wind, or to study the navigational charts unless they wished to wake up either the Captain or Barr.

The main worry at the back of Barr's mind was that the longer they stayed in the humid atmosphere of tropical waters, the more it would tell on Grant's cough and the more it would debilitate Lockyer. He had no idea of the ship's future role, but it was obviously something important, as a series of rather curious stores began to arrive aboard.

While ashore, Grant had managed to scrounge numerous coils of thick manila hawsers such as the *Carmania* used for warping herself alongside a pier. At least four inches thick and rock hard from disuse, an entire bargeload was delivered. After the hawsers came several thousand sandbags and a lighter load of sand, and finally a number of rolls of old steel-mesh torpedo nets, such as were used as a protection to hang over a ship's side or to guard the approach.channel of a harbor. At this time, as the thought of U-boats that far out in the Atlantic was unthinkable, Barr wondered what on earth his Captain was up to. He was soon to know.

The sandbags were to be filled and used as extra protection against the superstructure and to build a simple emplacement around the stern tiller and engine controls. The torpedo nets were suspended from wires rigged from the cargo derricks, forming a series of directional screens across the center of the *Carmania*'s broad decks. The derricks could be turned to deploy the screens in any direction. The surplus sand was tipped into the empty swimming pool. The hawsers were coiled and then used to festoon the bridge, so that they formed a primitive protection. By the time the complete installation was finished, the *Carmania* looked like a third-rate Christmas tree, and Barr devoutedly hoped to be out of Bermuda as soon as possible. He reckoned that the longer Grant remained ashore the more bits and pieces would be scrounged, and the *Carmania* would be so heavily laden that she would never clear the outward channel. Then, on the afternoon of August 28, he was surprised when a Marine orderly brought him an envelope. It was a formal invitation from Captain Grant, requesting his company at dinner at the Bermuda Yacht Club that evening. The card stipulated 7:30 P.M. for dinner at 8 P.M.

There had not been time to acquire formal naval evening dress before leaving Liverpool, so Barr donned his Cunard "mess kit," pinned his South Africa War medals on his lapel, tied on his crimson cummerbund, and around 6 P.M. went to board the duty boat that would take him ashore. He noticed that almost every other officer on the ship was similarly dressed and was waiting for him at the head of the gangway. As he went down to the duty boat, the Navy bosun's pipe shrilled its farewell, while the Marine sentries presented arms. Captain Grant was obviously planning a party, and for the first time since leaving Liverpool James Barr began to enjoy being in the Royal Navy.

At the same time, 2,500 miles to the south, Langerhannsz nosed the *Cap Trafalgar* gently into the dusk. At his masthead the signal flag D hung limply. This was his recognition signal, which was to be replaced by a signal light flashing the same letter once darkness fell. He was reluctant to use his lights, so, as he was some twenty miles short of the island, he decided to stay on the same course for another fifteen minutes, then heave to for the night. He was checking his watch to note the time when his masthead lookout reported to him that Trinidad Island lay ahead. Moments later came the flashing lights of the *Eber*'s challenge. The *Cap Trafalgar* identified herself, was acknowledged and, increasing speed, went forward to the rendezvous. She dropped anchor to the southwest of the island at almost exactly eight o'clock, probably as Captain Grant was leading his guests into dinner.

❧ 5 ❧

Grant had taken a private room for his dinner party. At the other end of the table he had placed Surgeon Commander Edwin Maynard. He was the *Carmania*'s peacetime medical officer, and together with the engineering department, he had accepted temporary rank in the Royal Navy Reserve. Grant, Commander Lockyer, and young Lieutenant Peter Murchie wore naval rig, lending a splash of color to the gathering. There were ten diners all told, nine from the *Carmania* and a reserved civilian who was introduced as Mr. Gordon.

Gordon sat to Grant's right, with Barr beside him. On Grant's left was the youngest midshipman, Douglas Colson, while the other guests were Lockyer, James O'Neill, who commanded the Marine infantry, Chief Engineer Francis Drummond, and his deputy James Macdonald. The tenth diner was the senior gunner from the regular Navy contingent, Henry Middleton. Middleton, who was not strictly an officer and technically should not, as a member of the "lower deck" have been in the club at all, was wearing a civilian dinner jacket, which the doctor realized almost certainly belonged to Lockyer. It was an unusual party, and Maynard, who had already come to the opinion that Grant was a rather unusual man, decided that he was going to enjoy himself.

He had no great expectations of the meal itself. Many

years at sea had taught him that the cuisine in any port that had been adapted to either a naval or a military palate suffered accordingly. The specter of chips, cabbage, and ketchup rapidly shriveled any native talent that might exist and corrupted local specialties. Maynard winced as he thought of the restaurants of Malta and Gibraltar. His problem was that he loved food, almost as much as he loved his fellow men.

Everyone observed the convention of not talking "shop" over the table. That would come later when the dishes were cleared and the port began to circulate. Instead, Grant began to draw people out, encouraged them to talk about themselves, to reminisce about their experiences at sea, their families, their interests, and their hopes for the future after the war.

Although he knew most of the men present fairly well, for he had been on the *Carmania* for almost two years, Maynard realized that he knew very little about them as personalities. In peacetime, he had his own table with the passengers. He was adept at spotting the bore, the hypochondriac, the likely coronary, or the drunk. He was aware that Lockyer was much too old to be at sea and that he had problems with his eyesight. He didn't believe for one moment that Grant had asthma, but neither did he believe that Grant would ever consult him, or, if he did, that he would pay any attention to his diagnosis and recommendations. Grant, he felt, sustained himself by sheer nervous energy. He looked at the jut of the jaw, then at the flush in his cheeks, the folds of skin on his neck and the backs of his hands. Grant, he reckoned, had lost over ten pounds in weight since he had joined the ship three weeks ago.

Grant was talking about Bermuda. Apparently he had spent 1908 as superintendent in charge of the dock establishment. He talked animatedly and with authority about the beauty of the island, the best places to go sketching, the difficulty of catching its peculiar light with watercolor. His conversation ranged to sketching in other far-off and exotic places where he had snatched painting holidays. In 1891 the Admiralty had actually paid for him to spend a holiday in Algiers provided his watercolors showed the fortifications of the port. Maynard joined in the approving laughter. The thought of the Admiralty actually paying for anything was a joke in excellent taste. Diagnostically, Maynard realized that Grant was now in his element, and Grant knew it himself. He was no longer an uninvited guest in another man's ship. He was on his home ground now and in his own way had decided the time had come to imprint his personality on the key members of the crew. Maynard realized why Noel Grant had commanded the battleship *Irresistible* at the age of forty-one. He also realized, as he watched his man toy with his food, why the command had only lasted a few months and had led to that long sketching holiday in Switzerland.

Midshipman Douglas Colson was rather unnerved sitting beside his Captain. He was being particularly careful not to talk until he was spoken to. He knew that the Navy regarded midshipmen as the lowest form of life and that this opinion was held unanimously from the scruffiest stoker to the Admiral of the Fleet. He was seventeen and barely six weeks ago had been an articled clerk in his uncle's solicitor's office in the sleepy cathedral town of Chichester in Sussex. He had put his name down for the Navy Reserve on his sixteenth birthday, merely because it was a method of getting some subsidized sailing. He had attended a weekly evening class in seamanship and had just finished his first two-week summer camp with the regular Navy when the test mobilization had been announced. Life on the *Carmania* was very different from what he had expected. There were three other midshipmen besides himself, and their main duties, apart from watchkeeping, were to command a boarding party if needed. It was an experience he dreaded and which he fervently hoped would never arise.

Grant rather liked young Colson. He was the undoubted ringleader in the midshipman's mess, and apart from his shyness, which was no drawback, he was careful and neat with his fingers when asked to do elementary navigational work, probably a legacy from his work as a solicitor's clerk.

A midshipman had to learn as he went along. He was treated as an officer by all aboard, though sometimes that respect would be difficult to discern. Henry Middleton, the chief gunner, for example, when explaining the intricacies of gun drill would work them hard, making them strip clean and reassemble the guns until they ached all over, remonstrating all the while. "You're a dunce—sir. You're idle—aren't you—sir?"

Just recently, Grant had chosen Colson to assist Lockyer on the gun control. It needed keen eyes and nimble fingers to work the rangefinder perched high on the top of the bridge. If the *Carmania* ever came to action, Grant wanted a younger man than Lockyer in that very exposed position.

Henry Middleton bulged out of his borrowed dinner jacket. He was fifty-five and had been in the Navy since he was sixteen. He had watched the Navy convert to steam and naval gunnery develop from an art into an exact science. He was a quiet, sturdy man, a total abstainer, which was a rare quality in those days, and at home in the village of Stoke Gabriel in Devonshire he had a wife and three daughters. His hobby was photography, and he had been delighted to find that the *Carmania* had a well-equipped dark room. Grant had noticed him eternally photographing his guns and gun crews, balancing an unwieldy tripod on the deck.

He had admired the way Middleton had integrated his

gunners into the ship's company, and, on their arrival in Bermuda, had listened carefully when Middleton, cap in hand, asked for an interview. It was Middleton's point that from a gunnery point of view the *Carmania* had grave disadvantages. He had not come to grumble; he had some positive suggestions to make.

He had explained that the shells for the guns were kept in the magazines down in the bottom of the ship. The hoist from magazine to deck was over seventy feet, and it was a simple affair of a rope and pulley, which could manage only two shells at a time. The magazine was located forward, and ammunition for the side and aft guns had to be carried by hand from the magazine hatch down the length of the deck. Middleton had suggested modifying the forward hoist, so as to bring up larger loads at a greater speed. It had also been his suggestion to build small caches of sandbags close to each gun in which to store ammunition for immediate use. Lastly he had suggested that they fill the swimming pool full of sand. His point was that there was too much wood around the *Carmania*. He didn't like to think about the consequences if there should be a breach burst or accidental fire on the foredeck. The ship was a tinder box, and if they went into action, fire would be their greatest enemy.

The ropes and screens had also been Middleton's idea. With ammunition stored on the deck, he had suggested them as a partial protection against splinters, not from shell splinters, he had hastened to add, but wood splinters. He had seen the havoc a bursting shell could cause to a wooden superstructure. It was the wood splinters that created carnage, not shrapnel. Grant had readily conceded all points, and it was Middleton whom Barr had to thank for the strange deliveries from the dockyard.

Peter Murchie, who sat on Maynard's left, was a career officer with the Cunard Company. In peacetime he had been

Barr's chief officer. He was a member of the Reserve, not from any particular wish but because it was part of Cunard's covenant with the British Government that, in exchange for a government subsidy, a proportion of all deck officers in the company's employment should be members of the R.N.R. When Grant and Lockyer had come aboard, Murchie had slipped slightly down the scale of command. He was a cheerful extrovert, forty years old, a bachelor, and he had already been earmarked by Cunard for command of one of their smaller liners. If war had not been declared, Murchie would probably soon have been a captain in his own right. His main responsibility was to work the ship and make the day-to-day decisions that did not require the Captain's imprimatur. When the *Carmania* went to action stations, Murchie had charge of the forward pair of starboard guns.

Barr spent most of the meal talking with his engineers. He realized as well as the doctor what Grant was up to, and entirely approved his action. He had no wish to try to steal the scene from him. Grant's guest of honor, Mr. Gordon, was on Barr's left and was a morose little man who concentrated on his food and did not bother to make conversation. Luckily for Barr, Francis Drummond, his chief engineer, was on his right, while Jamie Macdonald, who was Drummond's number 2, was opposite. Barr, who had spent his first twenty-five years at sea in sail, had a long-standing wrangle with them both that had been running in a good-natured fashion for a decade.

It was his contention that a man only became a seaman after a few years before the mast and that engines were dirty, smelly contraptions invented to give work to otherwise unemployable Scotsmen. He chaffed the engineers for making him clutter up the *Carmania*'s decks with coal and dust. In their turn, the engineers inevitably had their own back at Barr by talking between themselves just loud enough for Barr to hear. Drummond would remark that Cunard appeared to have adopted a policy of selecting their deck officers, particularly commanders, on the strength of their success with lady passengers. Macdonald would agree with him, then speculate how the little fellows managed to pit their charm against the big ones. Obviously they had to have something very special. Barr, who was the smallest of Cunard's captains, standing a stocky five feet four in his socks, accepted the badinage in the same way he had done for years. He was well aware that most of the engine room called him Smokey behind his back—not because of his pipe, but because he was always complaining that the boilers were fired too rich so that soot fell from the funnels onto the deck, and sometimes onto his passengers.

Barr was now thoroughly enjoying himself. He was launched into a thesis that the latest oil-driven turbines would breed a different class of engineers—men with whom one could afford to be seen in public, who could actually pass by anything shiny like a door knocker without whipping out an oily rag and trying to polish it—when he realized that the table had been cleared and the port was at his elbow. He filled his glass and passed the decanter to Gordon, who in turn passed it to Grant, thereby completing the round. The obligatory toast to the King was drunk, then Grant rose to his feet.

He explained that he had organized the dinner for three reasons. First, in some way he wished to say thank you to representatives from all parts of the ship for making his assumption of command of the *Carmania* such a pleasant experience. Second, he wished them all to meet and listen to Mr. Gordon, who would have a few words to say when he had finished, and it had seemed sensible that they meet Gordon here in the club. There were, he said, too many wagging tongues down on the dockside. Third, he wished to say something personal, something that had been on his mind ever since they had navigated their cautious way through the Bermuda channel.

He explained that twenty years ago, on August 28, 1894, he had been on the bridge of his first command. It was a small river gunboat called the *Linnet*. Working in the confined waters of the Peibo River, the *Linnet* had gone aground, a disgrace in the Navy second only to losing one's ship. He had been exonerated, but he knew that the fact that his ship had gone aground was on his record, and would be there forever. From then on, he explained, he had concentrated on being the best pilot and navigator that he could manage to be. Since that day twenty years ago, he had commanded destroyers, cruisers, even a battleship, but he wished everyone to know that the one fact he would like to be remembered for, of which he was most proud, was that he was "one of the men" who had managed to bring the *Carmania* into Bermuda. He felt that he had laid a ghost that had haunted him for twenty years, and he wished to thank everyone present. Tomorrow, he told them, they would make a double entry in the record book by taking the *Carmania* out again.

After some polite, but, as Maynard noted, slightly embarrassed applause, he introduced Mr. Gordon, who he said was "a special representative of the Admiralty."

Gordon didn't waste time. He explained that part of his job was to interview the masters of all ships passing through the port. He studied their manifests and bills of lading, then, after checking their statements as to what vessels they had seen on the voyage, he reported to the Admiralty. His concern was to gather information that might explain how the German cruisers and armed liners obtained supplies and fuel and in particular to discover how and where they transferred them. Coaling from one ship to another was a frightful task. It took time and needed a safe anchorage. Somewhere out on the

South American coastline there were several rendezvous. There must be because there were German ships still at sea whose bunkers should have been exhausted days ago.

He went on to explain the Admiralty's belief that a twin threat was developing, one to West Africa, another to the supply routes from South America. On August 16, he told them, the *Dresden* had stopped the S.S. *Siamese Prince,* an empty British cargo ship, searched it, and allowed it to proceed. The officer from the *Dresden* had signed the ship's log and explained that it was being allowed to go in the hope that the next time they caught her she would have a full cargo aboard.

Gordon was emphatic that the supply ships for Germany's commerce raiders had to be found and destroyed. An operation to do so was now in progress, under the command of Admiral Sir Christopher Craddock, Chief of the West Indies Squadron. However, the South American coastline was three thousand miles long and riddled with quiet inlets; he explained that this meant that Britain's cruisers conducting the search were also operating at the limit of their range. They also needed supply ships, and that was why the *Carmania* had been called in from the Atlantic Patrol. She was to sail tomorrow for Trinidad, West Indies, where she would be attached to Craddock's squadron as a supply ship and, if required, as a relief collier.

Barr nearly had an apoplectic fit on the spot. The *Carmania* a relief collier! Fortunately he kept his temper. Gordon asked if there were any questions. No one had any, so he bade them goodnight. A morose group of officers made their way back to their ship.

Feddersen had barely reported to his Captain that the *Cap Trafalgar* was anchored securely when one of the *Eber's* lifeboats drew alongside with a message from Captain Wirth.

It presented his compliments, cautioned the *Cap Trafalgar* to show no lights and to maintain steam so that she could get under way in a hurry, and included details of a further rendezvous if the ships at anchor had to disperse. Lastly, it informed Langerhannsz that Captain Julius Wirth of the Imperial Marine would board at 8 A.M. the following morning to formally assume command of the ship. Langerhannsz signed for the message, then scribbled a brief acknowledgment, saying that he looked forward to meeting Captain Wirth, and would be honored if he would be his guest for breakfast.

As Langerhannsz peered through the darkness he could see the dark shapes of several ships riding at anchor. Their numbers reassured him as he sat late in his cabin checking that all his ship's papers were in order. He knew the Imperial Navy to be sticklers for that sort of thing. Possibly he might have to do some explaining about his rather amateurish modifications, but he felt mightily relieved that he had safely brought the *Cap Trafalgar* to her rendezvous. He turned in that night, convinced that he and his ship were safe under the protective wing of the professionals.

Wirth was punctual to the minute, dressed in his best uniform, carrying his sword and his copy of the German Navy manual of officers' duties and responsibilities. He had been rather relieved to find that there was a section dealing with "taking over a new command at sea." It recommended a thorough inspection, rigid checking of all supplies, fuel levels, ammunition stocks, etc. It suggested a complicated procedure to settle disputes between the outgoing and incoming officers. In fact it was as prolix and detailed a manual as only a military bureaucrat of any nationality could devise. He fervently hoped that the outgoing fellow on the *Cap Trafalgar* wasn't a stickler for detail.

He expected to be met by a sentry at the gangway, greeted

with the appropriate naval honors, and escorted to the Captain. Bracing himself, he strode up the aft gangway, entering into the Winter Garden. There was no one about except Dr. Braunholz, who was feeding the parrots. Braunholz gave him a civil "Good morning" and went on with his work.

At that moment Langerhannsz came striding in, held out his hand, and said, "How nice to see you aboard, my dear fellow, my name's Langerhannsz."

Wirth sprang rigidly to attention, saluted and snapped out as smartly as he could muster, "Korvette Kapitän Wirth."

"Never mind all that," replied Langerhannsz, thankful that he had only a rather nice young man to deal with. "Put that frightening-looking cutlass somewhere and come and have some breakfast."

Clutching his sword, Wirth followed as Langerhannsz led the way through the Winter Garden. When Langerhannsz stopped by a large macaw, fumbled in his pocket for a nut, and gave it gingerly to the bird, Wirth stopped as well. He was beginning to feel slightly ridiculous. This tall, distinguished officer looked and behaved like a rather eccentric admiral. He decided to keep quiet about the list of questions he had prepared. Presumably Langerhannsz was the captain. The macaw having finished its breakfast, Langerhannsz set off again. Leaving the Winter Garden, they strode through the library and the smoking rooms, across the foyer, down the sweeping staircase to the vast dining room with its orchestra gallery at one end, and entered one of two smaller rooms that opened off it.

The table was laid for breakfast. Coffee percolated merrily over a spirit burner; baskets of fresh croissants and several types of bread still warm from the oven greeted him as did the smell from a series of chafing dishes; kidneys, bacon, and many other things simmered quietly beside an assortment of hams. The table seemed to be alive with fresh fruit. Oranges, melons, green figs, and bananas were heaped in a silver stemmed bowl in the center, while flowers floated delicately in the finger bowls beside each plate.

A steward took Wirth's cap and sword from him and vanished. Langerhannsz led his guest over to the sideboard, and Wirth helped himself with relish. He hadn't seen fresh bread since the *Dresden* had left or croissants since leaving Germany. For fully half an hour he totally forgot about the war as Langerhannsz discussed the weather, the shortcomings of his cooks, his plans for growing his own fresh fruit in the Winter Garden, and some of the less-endearing habits of the parrots. Each time Wirth looked up to speak, he was pressed to take more coffee, which a silent steward poured out for him. Langerhannsz had just finished an anecdote about his chef's efforts to make real Scots porridge when there was a knock on the door. Feddersen entered bearing a sealed message.

Langerhannsz took it, then, before he opened it, handed it to Wirth, suggesting that he had better have it as obviously he would deal with that sort of thing from now on. He introduced Wirth to Feddersen and then excused himself, saying that Feddersen would give him a tour of the ship, and perhaps if it was convenient, they could meet later on. Luncheon, he told the by now totally bemused gunboat captain, was served at noon in the main dining room. Until then he would be on the bridge.

Feddersen was a reserve officer and a thorough one. The guided tour that he gave Wirth missed nothing. They went down to the bowels of the ship. Starting from the bottom, he showed the new captain every cabin and compartment. As he went around he introduced him to the heads of each department, the engineers in the engine rooms, the bakers, carpenters, shipwrights, storemen—the list seemed endless. Wirth had seen service as a first lieutenant on a cruiser, but the *Cap Trafalgar* was larger and more luxurious than any ship he had ever been on. After weeks at sea, his feet felt leaden wading through the close-fitted carpets, while Feddersen's monologue had an almost soporific effect.

He was impressed by the turbine and propeller configuration, but before he could ask questions about them he was lost in a welter of details, ranging from the generating plant to the capacity of the fresh-water tanks. It was almost noon when they reached the bridge, and Wirth realized as he climbed the companionway that this was the first time since he had come aboard that he had been out on deck.

When they reached the bridge, Wirth stared in silent disbelief at the backdrop to the *Marriage of Figaro*. Langerhannsz asked him if he liked it, adding the bewildering comment that it was "a disguise knocked up in a day by the orchestra chaps." Wirth took a grip on himself, walked over to the bridge rail, and looked down on the blue-and-white-striped awnings that sheltered the foredeck from the sun. Looking fixedly out to sea he politely asked, "What armament do you carry, and where is it mounted?"

"Good God," exploded Langerhannsz, "you're as bad as the Argentines."

1. The *Carmania.*—Photo courtesy of the Cunard Company

2. The *Cap Trafalgar* in March 1914.—Hamburger *Freundenblat* 55, March 6, 1914

3. Captain Noel Grant, R. N. Photo by Chief Gunner Henry Middleton

4. Captain J. C. Barr. Photo by Chief Gunner Henry Middleton

Captain Julius Wirth in 1911.—
ndesarchiv

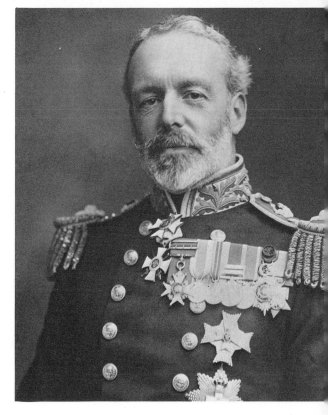

Admiral Sir Christopher Craddock.—
perial War Museum

7. One of Dr. Braunholz's pigs (note the parrot and the railway tie). The picture was taken on board the *Cap Trafalgar.*—Imperial War Museum

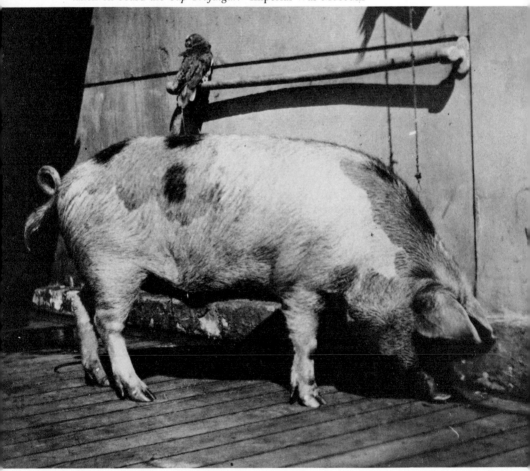

8. Rope protection against splinters on the *Carmania*. Photo by Chief Gunner Henry Middleton

9. The *Cap Trafalgar* at Trinidad Island, September, 1914, with the *Eber* alongside. Note that the rear funnel is missing.—Bundesarchiv

10. The *Carmania* approaching Trinidad Island. Photo by Chief Gunner Henry Middleton

11. The Bridge of the *Carmania* after the action. Surgeon Edwin Maynard is wearing the hat. Photo by Chief Gunner Henry Middleton.—Imperial War Museum

12. The *Carmania* undergoing repair at Gilbraltar in December, 1914. Photo by Chief Gunner Henry Middleton.—Imperial War Museum

›6‹

H.M.S. *Carmania* crept cautiously out of Bermuda during the morning of August 29. After an uneventful passage she docked at Trinidad, West Indies, on the morning of September 2, where she promptly refueled. Her cargo holds were loaded with coal and provisions, which she was ordered to deliver to Sir Christopher Craddock's squadron lying off the mouth of the Río de la Plata. She sailed at dawn on Friday, September 4.

Langerhannsz and Feddersen sat silently as they were rowed across to the *Eber.* Neither wished to speak in front of the boat's crew. It had been a traumatic and abrupt luncheon with Kapitän Wirth as matters had been explained to him. Feddersen had consoled himself that at least Wirth had approved of their efforts to disguise the ship and had even congratulated them on slipping out of Montevideo. Then Wirth had told them about the message that had arrived at breakfast. It was from the *Dresden,* ordering him to report the arrival of the *Cap Trafalgar* and confirm her availability for offensive action.

Wirth had then returned to his ship and asked them to join him for a conference at 4 P.M. He had asked them to bring a full crew list, together with details of the coal and provisions aboard. Feddersen had the papers with him and was not looking forward to the interview. One way or another he felt that Wirth blamed them for the whole chaotic state of affairs.

Langerhannsz took a more philosophical view. Privately he was convinced that the world had gone mad. He had liked Wirth, in fact, had felt desperately sorry for him. He was so keen, so eager, so transparently disappointed by the turn that events had taken. He had wanted to take the younger man to one side and comfort him. He could have sworn that when Wirth left for his own little gunboat he had been close to tears.

The issues they were now to discuss seemed very plain to Langerhannsz. Obviously there had been some ghastly mistake back in Berlin. It was idiotic even to try to make his ship into a cruiser. The sensible solution was for him to hand over all the coal and provisions he could spare, and then head for Pernambuco, where he could coal, and then with luck slip north to the United States. In his mind he started to calculate what he could spare the unfortunate Wirth. Coal, food, medical supplies, some comforts for his crew, perhaps some of the finer wines from his cellars. He brightened up at the thought that at least his owners would not grudge giving such a lonely and dedicated little naval crew a taste of luxury. He had been embarrassed by Wirth's hunger at breakfast. He would have the bakers working around the clock when he got back to the ship. He cursed himself for not thinking of it before. Obviously the poor fellows hadn't had fresh bread since they left Africa. He wondered if the *Eber* had a refrigerated room. He was still working out how he could help when they pulled alongside the gunboat.

They were greeted with full naval ceremony. A grave-faced lieutenant led them down to the wardroom, where Wirth had all his officers assembled. There were chairs around the table. Before each place was a note pad and pencil, a glass, and a carafe of water. The simplicity and the spartan appearance seemed to be a mute reproach to both the officers from the *Cap Trafalgar*. After formal introductions, Wirth asked them to be seated. He remained standing himself. Langerhannsz remembered that the thought flashed through his mind that he looked like a priest, or perhaps a saint.

Wirth began by surprising them. He congratulated both men in front of his own officers. Against great difficulties and in the face of a determined commercial and naval blockade, they had succeeded in carrying out their orders and delivered their ship to the appointed rendezvous at the appointed time. He wanted, in front of witnesses, to put his appreciation on the record. In due course, he would forward his opinions and his appreciation to Naval Headquarters. In the meantime, he would like to say that, on behalf of the officers and men of the *Eber,* he admired and was grateful to them.

Wirth sat down, drew his pad toward him and began to ask questions. Coal stocks? Range at what speeds? Type of radio installation? Height of the freeboard? Capacity of the holds? The list was endless and incredibly detailed. Fortunately both Langerhannsz and Feddersen knew their ship thoroughly, and could answer such *recherché* questions as to whether or not they carried welding equipment and the loading capacity of the cargo hoists.

Each answer was noted down, not only by Wirth but by some of the other officers as well. Then they in turn asked questions. The engineer asked the grade of lubricating oil, the navigator the range of charts carried, and what were the navigational aids used on board. When they had finished, Wirth asked Langerhannsz and Feddersen to withdraw for a few minutes. With a hint of a smile, he suggested they might care to take a tour of the ship, adding that it would not take very long and there was no chance of their getting lost.

Wirth then faced his own officers. He explained to them

that he had been ordered to assume command of the *Cap Trafalgar,* commission her for action, and embark upon a career of harassing the British merchant marine. They were all aware of the fact that the *Cap Trafalgar* was unarmed, which, though unexpected, was not the end of the world. He had decided that he would transfer the *Eber*'s armament and crew to the *Cap Trafalgar,* supplementing them as required with, he hoped, volunteers from the *Cap Trafalgar* herself and the colliers that were anchored nearby. He stressed that he was well aware that their initial armament would be puny, but as time went by, they might well rendezvous with other units of the German Navy and obtain guns from them. More likely, they might well fall in with an armed British merchant ship, which they must attempt to capture as a prize and seize the armament. The transfer of crews, coal, and weapons would begin at first light tomorrow morning. In the meantime, before nightfall, he wished the *Berwind* and the *Eleonore Wouvermans* to be warped alongside the *Cap Trafalgar*'s port side, and the *Eber* was to be placed against her starboard stern quarter.

There was just one point he wished to make before Langerhannsz and Feddersen returned. No matter how impractical any one of them thought the plan might be, they were to limit their reservations to discussion among themselves and with him. He stressed that the only way that they would all succeed and imbue those who volunteered or, if necessary, were conscripted with the confidence to make a success of their plan would be—or at least appear to be—totally confident themselves. On this note, he dismissed them, asking his second in command, Kapitän Lieutenant Erwin Rettberg to send his instructions to the masters of the *Berwind* and *Eleonore Wouvermans.* As the others withdrew, Langerhannsz and Feddersen re-entered the cabin.

Wirth briefly explained his plans to them. He asked them

to make ready to receive the two colliers. He suggested that the main dining saloon be used as a canteen and that some form of shift system be devised. Furthermore he would be grateful if accommodation could be provided for himself and his seven officers, including his doctor and his three engineering petty officers from that night. The following day he would need further accommodation for the remaining crew of the *Eber,* totaling 113. All carpets were to be removed, throughout the ship. They were to be rolled and together with all unused mattresses stacked inside the superstructure, particularly the Winter Garden, to form some sort of protection. This was to be done immediately, and he would expect to see it completed when he came aboard with his officers at 10 P.M. At 10:15, he wished to address the *Cap Trafalgar*'s crew in the main dining room.

Langerhannsz and Feddersen withdrew and rowed back to their ship. Langerhannz looked at his old command in a different light as they made their way to the wardroom. His eye caught one of the numerous portraits of Nelson's mobile sensitive face. Mentally he compared him to Wirth. Reassured, he turned to Feddersen and remarked, "That young man has found his Trafalgar."

"I think he's just written his own death warrant," replied Feddersen.

"That's what I meant," his former Captain replied.

When Wirth entered the dining room that evening it was packed. Everyone except the duty radio operator, engineer, and lookouts was present. The windows had been blacked out, the vast chandeliers switched down to half strength, but they still gave enough light for Wirth to see as motley an assembly of men as he, or the room, had ever seen. Stokers, seamen, chefs, greasers, and trimmers stood in a solid mass, which parted before him as Langerhannsz led him through the crowd and up onto the orchestra dais, where a long table had been set up with sufficient chairs for the officers from both ships. Langerhannsz briefly introduced Wirth, then sat down. Wirth came forward to the front of the dais and asked everyone present to sit on the floor.

His message was simple. The *Cap Trafalgar* was to be converted at once into a cruiser. This would mean that all those present were going to have to work harder than they ever had before, mostly at work they had never dreamed they would have to do. The next few days were going to be hot, dirty, and probably rather frightening. They all knew that the British cruisers were not far away, and he reminded them that, during the process of conversion, neither the *Eber* nor the *Cap Trafalgar* would be able to defend herself. When the conversion was finished, he would need additional men to work the ship. His own crew could fight it. He would need engineers, stokers, and deck seamen. He would need ammunition parties, fire parties, sick-bay attendants, and maintenance men. He would not require them all, and he was reluctant to forcibly recruit those that he did need as the Articles of War certainly entitled him to do. He explained that any person who felt that because of his conscience, his age, his health, from worry about his dependents, whatever the reason might be, was free to write his name, the department of the ship in which he worked, and his function, upon a piece of paper and place it in one of the numerous mail boxes that were scattered around the ship for the use of the passengers. These boxes would be cleared at midnight tomorrow. There was no reason to state the reason for not wishing to stay, but he reserved the right to refuse any application to leave, should that person's function be essential to everyone's safety. Lastly he explained that those who did leave would be transferred to one of the colliers alongside and put ashore at a neutral port. He realized that they were all civilians and had signed normal merchant

106

shipping articles. He assured them that the reason for their discharge from the *Cap Trafalgar* would not appear in their papers.

Wirth then asked Langerhannsz to explain the new administrative arrangements, which were basically who was to do what the following morning. Langerhannsz had divided the entire ship into two shifts, each working four hours, followed by four hours' rest and so on. During the rest period, men must get whatever sleep they could and take whatever they wished to eat. The main dining room would be open as a continuous cold buffet, with hot soup or coffee available twenty-four hours a day as from 4 A.M. the following morning.

Once the crew had dispersed, Wirth and Langerhannsz gathered their officers together and allocated the tasks ahead. The engineering officers of both ships took to each other at once, and without further delay they left for the engine rooms to be initiated into the mysteries of turbine propulsion and the other machinery aboard. The *Eber*'s first lieutenant, Gerhard Klevitz, paired up with Feddersen. Their job was to run the coaling operation, each in charge of separate shifts, and report to Langerhannsz, who would be responsible for the trim. Somehow or other they must devise a method of getting the coal out of the diminutive colliers into their own bunkers. If they needed to use the cargo hoists, then they must limit themselves to the use of those forward.

There were numerous other tasks to be planned. Water parties were to be sent ashore, together with all the firehoses that could be mustered from every ship anchored off the island. The ships' boats were to be stationed in a line at twenty-meter intervals, and the hoses strung between them. Water was then to be pumped from the shore into the tanks on first one ship then another until everyone's tanks were full. There was to be a twenty-four-hour lookout maintained on the top of the island and a system of signaling devised from hilltop to ship. Floodlights were to be rigged so that coaling could continue by night, Wirth relying on his lookouts to spot any approaching ships. A permanent radio watch was to be maintained on the frequencies known to be used by the British, and the *Eber*'s operator trained to operate the *Cap Trafalgar*'s installation. The list seemed endless, and it was dawn before the meeting broke up and each man went about his appointed task.

The main problem was the armament: first, to transship it, and second, where to place it. The *Eber* carried two 10.5-cm caliber breech-loading guns, each with a range of 7,000 yards. She also carried six 3.7-cm heavy machine guns. Wirth had planned to transfer the lot, but decided to leave one 10.5-cm on the *Eber* until all the others were installed, so that at least one of the craft under his command would have something to fight with.

The *Cap Trafalgar* had been built with four gun rings set into her decks, two forward and two on the afterdeck. These were simply reinforced sections of decking, each fitted with a revolving brass ring that lay flush with the deck and that spun on heavy-duty ball bearings. These rings were already drilled with holes so that her guns, which were still sitting in a warehouse in Hamburg, could be bolted on with a minimum of fuss. However, she had been designed for the latest type of 15-cm naval gun, and the bolt holes in her rings did not match the pivot bolts on the *Eber*'s older and smaller artillery. The first job was to drill a fresh set of boltholes through the five-inch-thick brass bases.

There were no mechanical tools suitable for the job on board either vessel, so they had to be drilled to a high degree of accuracy by hand, with drills whose bits were far too small for the job. Each hole, as it was finished, was reamed and filed so that the pivot bolts fitted absolutely tight. It was backbreaking, monotonous work, each hole—and there were sixteen per ring—taking over an hour to drill, with a team of men hand drilling as fast as they could for a few minutes at a time. The drilling started at 4 A.M. on August 29, and working two holes at a time, the men had modified both bases by shortly after noon.

While the bases were being adapted, work started aboard the *Eber* to remove her stern gun from its mounting and hoist it aboard. The *Cap Trafalgar*'s cargo hoists had a maximum lift of three tons, while the guns weighed almost four with their armor-plated shields. This entailed a certain amount of dismantling, and close maneuvering by the *Eber* so that she could place her stern immediately below the hoist cable. It called for precise ship handling, complicated by the fact that, while the *Cap Trafalgar* remained almost level in the swell, the *Eber,* as was her habit, seemed unable to keep still for a minute.

As this work went on, teams of men dismantled the machine guns and carried them aboard by hand. By noon they were being assembled on the deck. All that remained was to decide where to place them. This was the problem that worried Wirth most in the morning as he sat under the foredeck awning with the deck plans of the ship spread before him on a table. Beside him at another table sat Langerhannsz, busy with his loading tables as he decided where to store the coal that was being hauled aboard by the bucketload along a cable strung from the forward derrick, using the anchor winches for motive power. Wirth drew sketch after sketch of a bird's-eye view of the ship, then tried to calculate angles of fire. The difficulty was to find a series of fields of fire that were not obstructed by the cluttered superstructure. Langerhannsz watched him for a few moments, then shyly remarked, "You may not believe it, but I think I may be able to help you. I know quite a lot about the type of engagement I suspect you are planning."

Wirth laughed. "You're not that old, and I never knew the Hamburg South America Line employed pirates."

Both men were thinking along the same lines. They realized that if they should meet an armed adversary in a traditional ship-to-ship shootout, the *Cap Trafalgar* would be in a hopeless position. Her two small guns would be outranged by almost any armed merchant ship and every warship. Therefore it was essential to close up the range so that she could use her machine guns. Machine guns would be useless against the armor plate and gun turrets of a warship but would clear the decks of an armed merchant ship, whose guns would be unprotected on the open decks.

However, in using the machine guns, which had a maximum range of three thousand yards, the *Cap Trafalgar* would be suicidally close. The answer as both men saw it was to keep the enemy's head down with the machine guns until they could get men on board the enemy and capture her, together with her arms, coal, and ammunition. Langerhannsz voiced their mutual thoughts.

"You need a fire plan for close-quarter action against an enemy slower than yourself and to support boarding parties, am I right?" Wirth agreed. Langerhannsz suggested that they go into the library. He led the way and Wirth followed, carrying his pile of sketches. He sat down and listened patiently to the older man.

"Let's assume that you are approaching an enemy ship," began Langerhannsz. "Naturally you approach bow first, keeping as slim a profile as you can so as to offer as small a target as possible. When you wish to open fire, you do so with your two main guns, which I presume you're placing fore and aft." Wirth nodded. "Then one to port and one to starboard—

that way you will find that you can fire both guns forward if you alter your approach to a quarter profile. Look." He quickly drew arcs of fire on the plan.

Wirth watched entranced, then asked Langerhannsz how he knew this. Langerhannsz waved to the library shelves. "It's all there. I'm a Nelson student, and what you need here is what's called the 'Nelson Touch.'" He explained that this did not mean deliberate disobedience of orders as so many thought after Nelson turned his blind eye to his commanders' signals at the Battle of Copenhagen. It meant putting a boarding party onto the enemy. In Nelson's day, captains were grossly underpaid, and officers and crews were rewarded by "prize money" paid by their Admiralty for every ship, cargo, and prisoner they took. A captain without prize money could hardly afford to go to sea.

Wirth remarked that he was aware of the technique of making an attack the way that Langerhannsz had described. He had already calculated that before he ordered the gun bases to be redrilled. The problem was where to site the machine guns. Ideally they should be able to rake a ship as he approached and also give support to the boarding party as they went across from ship to ship. On something as maneuverable as the *Eber*, he could mount them on his flanks, because he could spin the *Eber* almost on her own length in an attempt to get alongside. With the *Cap Trafalgar* it was different. This time he took the pencil.

He sketched a diagram of two ships on a converging course. His forward 10.5-cm would fire when within range, concentrating at the bridge and radio installations. This would not be until he was within 7,000 yards. At 3,000 yards his machine guns would be effective. They too would concentrate on his opponent's upperworks. However, at his speed of, say 17 knots, and allowing the enemy 13 knots, the two ships would converge at a total speed of 30 knots. One nautical mile in just under two minutes. Did Langerhannsz follow his reckoning?

Wirth, acknowledging Langerhannsz's assent, went on to say that this meant that the obvious place for his machine guns was such that they did the maximum damage in as short a time as possible. He would have to put the *Cap Trafalgar* against the enemy bow on, as he had calculated that, given her size, she would take almost a mile to stop, and some three miles to curve around and come up side by side with the enemy.

Langerhannsz shook his head. The *Cap Trafalgar*, he claimed, was as maneuverable as the *Eber*, apart from being much faster. He explained the techniques of the triple screws and suggested that the machine guns be mounted at the bow on the starboard side and slightly aft of amidships on the port. Assuming that the point of boarding was to be level with the bridge the best technique to follow would be to try to lay the port forequarter alongside the enemy and then, using the flanking propellers, bring the stern in so that the ships would be locked side by side. As the boarders went across from below the port side of the bridge, the machine guns further aft on the port side would keep up continuous fire. He anticipated the question "Why the port side?" by explaining that, while the flanking screws turned in the opposite direction, the main screw turned the same way as the starboard. The resultant torque gave a natural port bias to the stern. Full speed astern on the main and starboard engines would snap her stern to port like a whiplash.

Wirth was almost convinced. Langerhannsz suggested that, since they had steam up, Wirth might allow him to give a demonstration.

The following morning, coaling was suspended as the *Eber* and the *Cap Trafalgar* put out to sea. After scouting around the island to see that no other ships were visible, they steamed in opposite directions until they were three miles apart, then, turning, made directly for each other as though they were knights jousting in some medieval tourney.

Langerhannsz and Wirth were on the *Cap Trafalgar*'s bridge. The *Eber* was commanded for the occasion by Erwin Rettberg. For the next few hours Julius Wirth was given a memorable lesson in seamanship, and Erwin Rettberg received an equally memorable series of frights of his life. Rettberg had been ordered to steer a course directly parallel to the *Cap Trafalgar*. On no account was he to divert from this until her bows were level with his, when he was to make as hard a turn to starboard as tight and as fast as the tired old hull of the *Eber* and sea conditions would allow. He was in fact nothing but a moving target, giving Langerhannsz a precise reference point moving at a series of different speeds.

The aim was to bring the *Cap Trafalgar* alongside an imaginary ship that was exactly behind the *Eber*, so that if the *Eber* had been their own size, they would achieve the optimum boarding position. The turn to starboard was a safety precaution to prevent the *Eber* from being swamped or capsized as the great propellers of the larger ship went suddenly into full astern. When the technique was used in action then the vortex would draw the enemy into them.

On the first run, Langerhannsz took the wheel himself, braced his feet, and squinted down the foredeck to the *Eber* creaming toward him. He wondered briefly what his board of directors would say if they could see him now, then concentrated as the *Eber* suddenly began to loom larger and larger. When he was two of his own ship's lengths away, he snapped the order to full astern all engines; then as the stern tried to veer to port he held her steady until the *Eber*'s topmast slipped past his bow. As it did, he nodded to Wirth, who rang half ahead of the port turbine control as Langerhannsz spun the wheel to starboard as fast as he could.

113

The *Cap Trafalgar* shuddered in protest as she began to slue seemingly out of control almost on top of the *Eber*, which was visible beneath the port rails. All Langerhannsz and Wirth could see was her topmast as it hurtled by them, seemingly within touching distance. The *Eber* slid out from beneath the overhang of the *Cap Trafalgar*'s stern, shook herself free from the maelstrom of water thrown up by the screws, and continued her starboard turn.

All that day the two ships played their astonishing game of "chicken," the *Cap Trafalgar* playing a twenty-thousand-ton projectile, the *Eber* the target. When Langerhannsz was sure that Wirth had mastered the technique for an attack on a converging course, he handed command over to him. When Wirth was satisfied, he would hand it back, and a practice on a different direction-of-attack approach would begin. They practiced attacks from each quarter and from right angles. When they felt they had mastered them, they began all over again.

Communication during the day had been entirely by signal lamp and semaphore. As dusk fell, Wirth ordered a return to the island. However, the strain had taken its toll of the little *Eber*, and she signaled that she had lost boiler pressure and was taking water through her propeller shafts. Reducing speed eased her trouble, but it was dawn on August 31 when they anchored once more beside the two colliers.

The day's respite for the men loading coal had been expensively bought, for that day consumed almost two hundred tons and, working round the clock, they could load only about one hundred tons a day. The following morning, work started again. The other gun was winched up from the *Eber* and installed on the port side of the foredeck. The machine guns were sited as Langerhannsz had suggested and according to a sketch made by Wirth (see illustration).

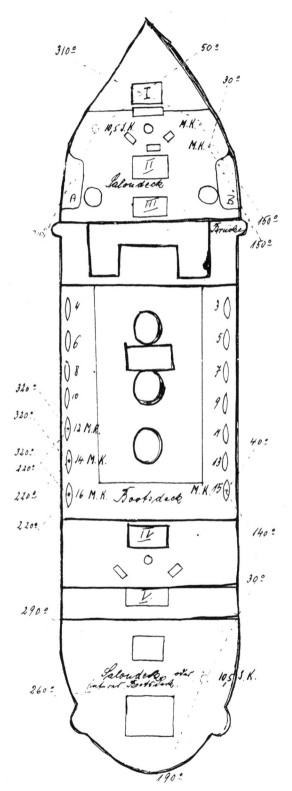

Diagram of the CAP TRAFAL-
GAR drawn by Captain Wirth
at Trinidad Island, August 31,
1914. Captain Wirth gave it to
Langerhanz, who in turn gave
it to the German Legation in
Buenos Aires September 24,
1914. -- Bundesarchiv, Cob-
lenz

Key:

MK = machine gun

10.5cm (4.1") SK = quick firing deck gun

The roman numerals indicate
the hatch covers where ammunition was stored.

Arabic numerals indicate the
angles of fire allocated to
each gun position, and where
they are beside little drawings
of life boats, the numbers of
each life boat station. The
letters A and B relate to the
boarding platforms. Hatch II
is the site of the first boarding party. The German text
at the bottom of the diagram,
near the stern, means saloon
deck or afterboat deck.

Four were mounted on the after end of the boat deck, three to the port side, one to starboard. The remaining two were placed on the starboard side of the saloon deck immediately below the bridge, and level with the port-side 10.5-cm. By judicious siting, fairly wide arcs of fire were achieved. Their maximum traverse was 200 degrees, but this was only possible in the case of the forward gun on the starboard side. The others had an average arc of 100 degrees before there was a danger of shooting up either another gun or a part of the ship.

The two 10.5-cm were technically capable of firing through a full circle of 360 degrees, but, as Wirth's diagram shows, the superstructure and the masts deprived the aft gun in particular of a vital forward arc of 40 degrees. More important, in the case of a frontal attack, the *Cap Trafalgar* would have to expose her high and vulnerable sides at an angle of at least 30 degrees to the enemy if the aft gun was to be brought into action.

By the afternoon of September 3, the *Eber* had been gutted of all her naval equipment except the bare necessities for navigation. The last item to come aboard was her searchlight, which was screwed to the *Cap Trafalgar*'s navigation bridge. Julius Wirth went aboard his little ship for the last time, looked around for a moment at his deserted cabin, then took a package from his locker and climbed briskly up the companionway onto the deck. He paused, stood at salute for a long moment, then, still holding his package, rejoined the *Cap Trafalgar*. All that she needed now he held in his hand: one brand-new battle ensign of the Imperial Navy.

❧7❧

During the evening of Thursday, September 3, both British and German radio operators were busy. The German network, controlled from their communications center in New York, sent a stream of instructions via their legations and consulates to the numerous cargo ships hovering in South American ports. At Pernambuco, the steamers *Prussia* and *Ebenberg* were ordered to sail for Trinidad to rendezvous on September 14 with the *Cap Trafalgar* and the *Kronprinz Wilhelm.* The *Corrientes*, lying in Rio, was ordered south to Bahía Blanca; during the voyage she would be contacted by the *Karlsruhe*, to which she would deliver supplies. The *Santa Lucia* and the *Santa Isabel*, which were lying empty off Trinidad Island, were ordered to Rio to recoal, while the *Pontos* and *Eleonore Wouvermans* were to remain at Trinidad to supply the *Dresden*, which was expected at any time. The *Berwind*, which the German Admiralty believed to be empty after recoaling the *Cap Trafalgar,* was ordered to Montevideo and thence to obtain clearance for New York. The *Cap Trafalgar* was to sail when ready and attempt to destroy British shipping heading north from Montevideo. She was also to reconnoiter the island of Rocas off the Brazilian coast to see if it was suitable for use as an alternative rendezvous.

Unfortunately, the *Berwind* was still heavily loaded. She

had found it almost impossible to get her coal up onto the *Cap Trafalgar*, and the heavy swell had repeatedly slammed her against the sides of the larger ship. When Wirth summoned all the collier masters aboard to give them their orders, the *Berwind*'s master explained that his ship was taking too much water through her buckled plates to even attempt the trip to Buenos Aires. He needed time to clear his coal and effect rudimentary repairs.

Wirth disliked the man. He regarded him as a trouble-maker. The incident of the Spanish firemen had been stupid and unnecessary; neither did he like the idea of either the *Berwind* or her crew talking along the Montevideo waterfront. He ordered the *Berwind* to transfer her cargo to the *Pontos* and *Eleonore Wouvermans* and then return directly to New York. He suspected, and he was probably right, that if he allowed the *Berwind* to sail to Montevideo, her master would take advantage of the *Cap Trafalgar*'s absence, find a suitable excuse for not transferring his coal to the other colliers, and head directly to Montevideo to sell it at an inflated price.

The problem was that the *Berwind*, though technically under his command, also had a direct link with the German naval attachés in America. She had unusually sophisticated radio equipment, and her officers were not exactly profes-sional merchant seamen. Wirth regarded them as both ama-teurs and adventurers and suspected their loyalties lay nearer to the easy dollar than to the Fatherland. For the time being, he could do little more, except neutralize them and their ship until they were ready to sail for New York.

The collier masters had hardly left when the lookouts signaled smoke on the horizon. Wirth sent an officer up to confirm, but when he arrived there was no sign of a ship. Nevertheless it unsettled Wirth, who was beginning to regard Trinidad as both unsuitable and insecure. He decided to search for another base in the morning, but there was still a considerable amount to do.

He had delegated the sorting out of the crews to Feddersen and the *Eber*'s senior lieutenant, Gerhard Klevitz. They had decided to retain all of the *Cap Trafalgar*'s engineers and engine-room staff, who had volunteered to a man. In fact there had been fewer than thirty requests to be relieved. The *Cap Trafalgar* had left Montevideo with 279 men aboard, compared to her usual complement of 430. Seven officers and 170 of the crew were chosen to remain aboard. They were joined by all of the *Eber*'s officers and petty officers, together with 113 out of her crew of 131. The *Cap Trafalgar*'s new operational crew was now 13 officers, 5 petty officers, and 283 men, totaling 301.

Wirth scanned the list of 102 men who were to be transferred to the *Eber*. Most of them were either elderly or suffering from some minor injury, for the conversion had taken a heavy toll in crushed fingers and strained backs. The *Cap Trafalgar*'s doctor insisted on staying with the sick, but that presented no problem as he had his own doctor aboard from the *Eber*. The only name on the list that surprised him was that of Langerhannsz. He immediately sent for him.

Langerhannsz explained that there could be only one captain of a ship at a time, and he felt that his presence might cramp Wirth's style. However, he had no wish to be sent off to internment in some neutral port. He had begun to enjoy himself as a temporary Navy man. He would be most grateful if Wirth could find him some suitable employment. Wirth had no hesitation. He immediately placed him in overall command of the civilian ships and the small shore establishment on the island and suggested that he join him for a talk later that evening when the crew transfers had been completed.

Those selected to leave the ship carried their possessions

119

aboard the *Eber.* Second Officer Bunte, whom Langerhannsz had borrowed from the *Camerones* while in Montevideo, was placed in command of the little gunboat and told to sail the next morning for Bahía Blanca. He was to take care, instructed Wirth, not to arrive before the night of September 13.

The reason for this was that although the *Eber* was no longer a warship she was likely to be regarded as one for at least a few days. The international convention regarding warships entering neutral ports was that they had to have an excellent reason to do so, such as unseaworthiness or an epidemic or such aboard. Unless concessions were made at the highest level, the warship would have to leave after twenty-four hours had elapsed. Wirth calculated that if the *Eber* arrived on the 13th she could not be interrogated until early on the 15th, and therefore, if the use to which Trinidad was being put was discovered, then he would have until probably about September 17 before it would have to be abandoned. That would give both the *Cap Trafalgar* and the *Kronprinz Wilhelm* time to keep their rendezvous on the 14th, rebunker, and move off to another rendezvous.

Langerhannsz moved his kit across to the *Eleonore Wouvermans* and confirmed that he would come back aboard later on in the evening. Wirth, who by now was extremely fond of the older man, could not resist his teasing rejoinder. "No, no, have an early night, dear ancient mariner, but I should be honored if *you* would be *my* guest for breakfast in the morning."

The spate of German cables had been intercepted as they were transmitted, and the tenor of them indicated that Sir Christopher Craddock's squadron was to have its hand full. An analysis of them was telegraphed by the Admiralty to Naval Headquarters, West Indies, and arrived on the morning of September 4, shortly after the *Carmania* had cleared harbor on her supply mission. The Admiralty analysis remarked upon the fact that most German collier traffic seemed to have an average voyage length of twelve days between leaving port with full cargoes and arriving at another port either empty or in ballast. Assuming that they were refueling the enemy at sea, and in light of the weather conditions that had been prevailing, such as the heavy swell, together with the known time that it took to transfer coal from one ship to another, the logical deduction was that they were effecting their transfer very close to either their port of origin or their port of arrival. In view of the weather the Admiralty believed the refueling was carried out in some sheltered bay. Another alternative was that they had a permanent fuel base on some likely island, where they could leave their cargoes to be collected later. The flag officer, West Indies, was instructed to order a search of all such islands in his operational area.

The Admiralty instruction also respectfully drew attention to the fact that many islands that were too small to be charted except on the largest charts might well be capable of being used by the Germans. It drew attention to the fact that what some people called an island others merely referred to as a navigational hazard—such as a rocky outcrop, coral outbreaks, even sand bars that might be partially submerged at high water. Even these, it said, were capable of hiding drums of diesel oil, for example.

The phrase "navigational hazard" struck a chord in the mind of Lieutenant Commander Goodwin, R.N., who held the post of dispatching officer at Naval Headquarters, West Indies. His function was to brief every outward-going ship as to the latest information on the believed whereabouts of German commerce raiders. One of his lesser duties was to ensure that their charts were marked with the latest information, such as minefields, wrecks, and other "navigational hazards." The evening before he had briefed the *Carmania* before she left Trinidad, West Indies, and had accepted an invitation to stay for dinner in the wardroom. Captain Grant had unfortunately been indisposed, but Commander Barr had been a delight to listen to, particularly his stories of his experience in South American waters before he joined Cunard in 1885.

Goodwin tried to recall some of the things Barr had said over the dinner table. He could remember such facts as that Barr had first rounded Cape Horn when he was seventeen and that he had been shipwrecked three times in South American waters before he joined Cunard as a young deck officer. Barr had been scathing about the way the Latins had maintained their navigational marks. Lights were inaccurate, danger buoys wrongly placed, soundings inaccurate.

The best tip after rounding the Horn and clearing the Falklands had been to stay as far away from the South American coast as possible. The trade winds would constantly try to drive a ship onto a lee shore. His own formula for survival for the long haul to the north was to steer for the Vas Rocks. There was an island nearby with a reasonable anchorage. His last visit had been in 1884. There had been fresh water and a colony of Scotsmen trying to cultivate castor-oil plants. Goodwin remembered someone or other had made a bawdy joke about castor oil and sailing ships.

He opened up his gazetteer and checked the Vas Rocks. Once he had found their position, he started to measure off distances with a pair of dividers and compare them with the known dates of arrival and departure of German colliers. The rocks were a possible bet. Even more likely was the little island of Trinidad some thirty miles to their west and closer to South America. Without giving the matter a second thought, he added their names to the list of possible places to be checked by Craddock's cruisers; then, from force of habit, he marked them on his master chart as an area likely to be either a navigational hazard or frequented by Germany's commerce raiders.

Captain Grant's indisposition was not at first very much of a strain. The *Carmania* ran as always like clockwork. There was little to do except rig the sun awnings and keep a sharp lookout. The weather was humid to the point of discomfort, often with a heat haze by day and mist by night. The *Carmania*'s instructions were simple enough. She was to proceed to the Río de la Plata, keeping approximately one hundred miles off the South American coast. She was to maintain a permanent listening watch on her radio and use her own only in emergency or in making a challenge to unknown ships. All British cruisers in the area had been advised of her voyage, and they would signal her, not she them.

The British patrol areas off South America were roughly the same as those around the British Isles. Each cruiser patrolled a rectangle stretching from the limit of territorial waters to some fifty miles out to sea, and covering a length of coastline approximately one hundred miles long. Within these areas, British and French shipping moved in procession, responsibility for the ships being handed over from one patrol area to another by the shepherding cruisers. To seaward, their presence formed a barrier to marauders like the *Cap Trafalgar* and her sisters. From the shore, their presence was a constant threat to the blocked German colliers, whose only recourse was to try to slip down the coast through territorial waters by night, lying up in some remote and friendly cove by day.

On September 7, the *Carmania* was due to rendezvous with the cruiser *Cornwall* off the tiny Brazilian island of Fernando de Noronha, which lies some three hundred miles northeast of Pernambuco. She approached from the west through a thick sea mist. Because of the mist Barr decided to give a wide berth to a lonely outcrop called Rocas that lay between Fernando and the coast.

The *Carmania* passed some twenty miles north of Rocas at the same time as Wirth in the *Cap Trafalgar* approached it from the south. His mission was to see if it was suitable as an alternative to Trinidad. If the *Cap Trafalgar* had continued her course to the north, then she and the *Carmania* would have met a week earlier than fate intended. As it was, and from the two steamers' track charts, they passed later that evening within firing range of each other, each hidden by the combination of darkness and mist.

The *Carmania* never kept her rendezvous with the *Cornwall*. Shortly after leaving Rocas to her starboard, she received a signal to divert immediately to lie off Pernambuco, where the German colliers *Prussia* and *Ebenberg,* taking advantage of the weather, had slipped out on their way to meet the *Cap Trafalgar* at Trinidad. The *Cornwall* had missed them in the fog, and signaled the *Carmania* to act as a backstop. Barr brought his ship around and, steaming as fast as he dared, took a course that took him between Fernando and Rocas. The *Cap Trafalgar* picked up the *Cornwall*'s signal. She had no way of knowing what it meant, only that it came from within a radius of a hundred miles. Moments later she heard the *Carmania*'s acknowledgment.

The *Carmania* had been allocated the identity prefix of Q.T. She also had an exceptionally powerful transmitter. When Wirth heard her signal, although he had no idea who she was, it appeared from the signal strength that she was almost on top of him. Wirth stopped all engines. The *Cap Trafalgar* lay motionless in the mist, but she could hear nothing. In fact, the *Carmania* passed about three miles away as she steamed down to Pernambuco. The *Cap Trafalgar* lay hove to until dawn, listening in to the crackle of the British radio messages as the hunt for the two colliers intensified. At dawn on September 8 he circled Rocas, noted an anchorage that might be suitable, then headed due south on his return leg to Trinidad. His course took him parallel with the eastern or farthest seaward boundary of the patrol areas assigned to Craddock's cruisers. The volume of radio traffic convinced him that he was wasting his time trying to find a substantial victim, on whom he could attempt the "Nelson Touch." He decided that his most intelligent course was to keep his rendezvous at Trinidad for the 14th, then sail southward, and try to establish a base nearer Cape Horn, or even, if necessary, round the Horn and join up with the German Pacific Fleet.

Unaware of the *Cap Trafalgar*'s presence, Barr pushed the *Carmania* through the mist toward Pernambuco. Grant was still in his cabin, and Lockyer, technically the second in command, was only too content to let Barr handle the ship in the difficult conditions. He reasoned very sensibly that Barr knew these waters and the ship better than anyone else. Barr, delighted to be in charge of his own bridge again, decided to spend the night with the watch. In the early hours, he was joined by Surgeon Commander Maynard, who asked for a word with him. Cautioning the lookouts to call him if required, Barr led the surgeon into the chart house and closed the door.

Maynard came straight to the point. Grant was not only a very sick man, he was in Maynard's opinion a dying man. The fact that he had survived so long was due more to willpower than anything else. The trouble was tuberculosis, not only of the lungs but of the bones as well. There was nothing he could do for him, except prescribe total rest and immediate evacuation from the humidity and coal dust. Barr asked him how sure he was of his diagnosis. Could Grant's fever not be a touch of malaria? His cough, the result of the coal dust and the switch from the cool breezes of the North Atlantic to the present humidity and discomfort? Maynard was unable to answer. He explained that he had mentioned the matter to Barr because he still thought as a civilian doctor speaking to a civilian captain. He admitted that without recourse to the sophisticated equipment that a hospital could provide he would be reluctant to go against the Navy surgeons who had presumably certified Grant fit before he assumed command. Nevertheless he felt that Barr should know the situation.

Barr reflected for a moment. He was steaming through darkness and thick mist, hoping to intercept the two enemy colliers. Somewhere out in the darkness was the *Cornwall.* At this moment he was unable to make up his mind whether she was of any use to him or a collision hazard, but at least she would have a doctor on board. There was, he reflected, the chance for a second opinion, but at the moment there was little point in doing anything, except, of course, telling Maynard to make his patient as comfortable as possible.

He asked Maynard how Grant would be in the morning. He was surprised to learn that Grant might very well appear to be perfectly all right. He would, of course, feel weak, but he would never show it. Maynard explained that he had discovered that Grant had been concealing his cough. It had, he said, been Grant's steward who had consulted him, when he had noticed Grant's pillows and bed linen spattered with blood in the mornings. Grant, it appeared, had not formally consulted him at all. On hearing that he was unwell, Maynard had looked into his cabin as a matter of courtesy and found him with a high fever and semi-conscious. He had examined him while in this condition. Grant had made no objection. He had been in no state to do so even if he had felt like it. Maynard added that he thought that this might well not have been the first time that Grant had collapsed. There had been other times when he seemed to have spent considerable periods alone in his cabin. It was possible that he would awake refreshed, then drive himself for a few days until he collapsed again. Each time, the intervals between collapse would get shorter and shorter. Leaving Barr with this somber thought, Maynard excused himself and left the chart house.

Barr went out onto the bridge. Dawn was breaking through the mist and the watches were changing over. Within a few minutes Lockyer joined him, and a steward brought them both mugs of coffee. Lockyer seemed to regard Barr as the natural Captain. He made no mention of Grant, but suggested to Barr that it would be prudent to send the gun crews to action stations, explaining that if the mist cleared they might just find the two German colliers alongside. Barr agreed, and asked Lockyer to get his crews up to their guns as quietly as possible. It was not that he wished to avoid disturbing Grant's sleep. He believed that at this hour of the morning, and in this mist, any sound, let alone the clang of gongs and bells ringing for action stations would carry for miles. If the fog siren was forbidden on operational patrol, then surely the alarm bells were as well.

Quietly and without fuss, the gun crews went to their stations. The ammunition and fire parties took up their positions, bulkheads were closed up, and the marines formed up on the boat deck. Lockyer and young Colson climbed up to their fire-control position and Lieutenant Battle took up his emergency station by the aft tiller control. Barr picked up the voice pipe and, whistling softly down it, brought an answering grunt from Chief Engineer Drummond. He asked for plenty of steam to be ready in case it was needed. The sun was now up over the horizon and its first rays began to disperse the mist. Visibility slowly increased. The lookout, high on the foremast, could now see over the mist that curled up from the waves then slowly evaporated in the sun. Suddenly his voice rang out with the cry that Barr had been half expecting, "Smoke."

From the bridge, neither Barr nor the watch could see anything. However, Barr knew what to do; he had practiced it a hundred times under Grant's tutelage. He now had to make the ship's challenge. This was a complicated coded signal that identified himself and at the same time asked the other ship who and what she was. The challenge varied for each day of the week and in each different patrol area. The time of change-over was midnight. After he had given the order to the signalers to challenge with radio and searchlight, Barr realized too late that they had only the code for the previous day. The challenge for Tuesday, September 8, was locked in Grant's safe. Normally it would have been handed over when watches changed during the night.

Barr knew he could not leave the bridge. He hesitated for a moment, then decided to wake Grant up. He pushed the button that sounded "action stations" throughout the ship. He knew perfectly well that there was an alarm bell over Grant's bed. Within a minute, Grant lurched onto the bridge, dressed in his pajamas, with a polka-dot dressing gown flapping from his shoulders. Barr shouted to him to get the challenge book, but Grant appeared not to hear him.

With Grant now on the bridge, and technically in command, Barr wasted no more time. He ran down to Grant's cabin, found his keys on the bedside locker, and opened the safe. Grabbing the signal books and leaving the safe open, he ran back to the bridge. Within two minutes of Grant's appearance, the correct challenge was being flashed out by searchlight and radio operators. Barr could now see the smoke on the horizon silhouetted against the rising sun. He waited anxiously. He was more worried that it was the *Cornwall* than an enemy.

The *Cornwall* was under instructions, as were all Craddock's ships, that any strange ship was an enemy, unless the approaching ship identified herself. The onus was upon the

Carmania to show who she was, and the *Cornwall*, in the absence of a sign of friendship from the *Carmania*, would not hesitate to open fire.

Above his head, Midshipman Colson was calling out the range between the two ships. His first figure was 16,000 yards. Barr knew that the *Cornwall* had fourteen six-inch guns with a range of around 13,000 yards. In about two minutes she would be able to open fire. Colson now called the compass bearing of the smoke, which was some 40 degrees to starboard. Barr decided to make the *Carmania* as small a target as possible, and to gain some time before the *Cornwall* came into firing range. He gave the order to the helmsman to steer to starboard and hold the *Carmania* so that she was bow onto the approaching ship. At the same time he called down to the engine room to reduce speed. He calculated that his speed reduction would gain him a couple of extra minutes. Lastly he shouted to the signalers to repeat the challenge.

Grant had moved directly behind him. In a soft voice he whispered into Barr's ear. "I would thank you, Commander, to allow me to give my own orders. Report to the aft control." Before Barr could reply, the signaler came running up to them. He said, "Message from *Cornwall*, sir," and handed the paper to Barr. Grant snatched it from him, opened it, and read it. Quietly he ordered full ahead. Barr saluted and went to his position at the aft control.

He was angry, he was hurt, and he would have dearly loved to see the *Cornwall*'s message. It read: "If at first you don't succeed try and try again."

8

Captain Ellerman of H.M.S. *Cornwall* had a reputation in the Royal Navy as a humorist. His message to the *Carmania* was entirely in character,* and it is unlikely that he would have fired at her anyhow. As far as he was aware, there was no other ship of the *Carmania*'s size in those waters, except of course the *Trafalgar*, which both Ellerman and the Admiralty firmly believed to have escaped to the west coast of Africa. Furthermore, with the rising sun behind her he had been able to identify the *Carmania* without difficulty. He was an acquaintance of Grant's and no doubt looked forward to meeting someone relatively fresh out of England with all the latest news.

This was not to be. As the two ships closed on each other, a typical Atlantic heavy swell worked up, making it impossible either to go alongside or even to lower a boat. Their communication was entirely by signal lamp and semaphore.

The *Carmania* was told that, as weather conditions made it impossible to transfer either water or coal, she was to proceed to the mouth of the Río de la Plata, where she was to

---

* The probably apocryphal story is told that during the Royal Review of the Fleet in 1912, Ellerman's ship was grazed on the stern by the Royal Yacht. Ellerman promptly hoisted a flag signal that read, "If you touch me there again I shall scream." The King was greatly amused. The signal defused what could have been a career-wrecking situation for the captains of both ships.

rendezvous with the cruiser *Glasgow*. She was also told to keep well to the east of the patrol area and make her passage south, standing at least two hundred miles out to sea. As she would then be in unpatrolled waters, she was to report her position by radio every six hours. She was also given a list of British cargo ships in the area through which she would pass, and told to keep a sharp lookout for the elusive German colliers. Once the *Carmania* had acknowledged her instructions, the *Cornwall* resumed her patrol.

Both Grant and Barr regarded the new instructions as a reflection on their ability to take the *Carmania* through the patrol areas without causing confusion and possible havoc among the cruisers and merchantmen there.

Grant ordered the ship's company to leave their battle stations, handed the watch over to Murchie, and retired to his cabin. Shortly afterward, he handed out a new set of officers' duties. Basically the watches were to be shared between Lockyer and Murchie, who were to report directly to him. Barr was asked to abandon watchkeeping and to concentrate on the duties of navigating officer and the correlation of intelligence. It was a blow to his pride, and an uncomfortable one as well, for it entailed his living and sleeping in the chart house beside the bridge, but with no responsibility for the operation of the ship.

Any chance of receiving a second opinion on Maynard's diagnosis had evaporated with the *Cornwall*'s departure. It would be at least another three days before their rendezvous with the *Glasgow*, and there was nothing Barr could do except hope that nothing happened to complicate his difficult position further.

Both men misinterpreted the reason for the change of plan. It was no reflection at all on either their ability or their seamanship. They would have been given precisely the same instructions, even if they had managed to challenge the

Cornwall correctly. The diversion to the seaward side of the patrol area had been caused by events completely outside their control. The same instructions had been given to all other ships engaged on similar errands as themselves. The reasons were tactical, and to understand them at this remove, the overall picture of the game of naval chess being played in South American waters must be examined. This examination, to be fair to all concerned, must contain no element of hindsight, for that has been the curse of official historians, both British and German, when they cover this period.

During the first month of the war, in the waters of the Atlantic between South America and Africa, and bounded by the West Indies and the Azores to the north and the Atlantic to the south, the only regular units of the German Navy were the light cruisers *Dresden* and *Karlsruhe*, together with the gunboat *Eber*. There were also the auxiliary cruisers *Kronprinz Wilhelm*, which Craddock had surprised being armed by the *Karlsruhe*, the *Cap Trafalgar*, and the *Kaiser Wilhelm der Grosse*, which had broken out of German waters into the Atlantic and had been sunk by the *Highflyer* on August 26.

The *Carmania*'s revised instructions were given to her on September 8, which had allowed ample time for the news of the *Highflyer*'s success to be received, published, and analyzed. The German Admiralty knew that their sole remaining strength in the South Atlantic was the *Dresden, Karlsruhe, Kronprinz Wilhelm,* and *Eber*, all of which were armed. Some sections of the German Admiralty believed the *Cap Trafalgar* was armed as well. The German plan was that these ships should sit astride the trade route from the Plata and cause as much havoc as possible.

The trade route from Brazil was vitally important to Britain. Both in the number of ships and the tonnage carried, it was more important than the combined trade from India, Australia, New Zealand, and the eastern seaboard of the

United States. It was Britain's prime source of meat and leather, with which to feed and equip her armies, and nitrates and copper for munitions. The British Fourth and Fifth cruiser squadrons were assigned to protect this vital artery. These two squadrons were under the overall command of Rear Admiral Sir Christopher Craddock, an impetuous but gallant officer of considerable seniority. With his neatly trimmed gray beard and flowing mustaches and shirtful of decorations for chivalry and long service in distant waters, he was an imposing and frightening figure. He had these disadvantages. His ships were old. They were far too few to cover the thousands of miles of ocean under his aegis. And, in common with most of his contemporaries, he had never fired a shot in anger, except while bombarding some distant native shore settlement in support of the Pax Britannica.

Apart from the marauding German commerce raiders, Craddock had a further worry. Somewhere within a thousand miles of Cape Horn were the two German battle cruisers *Scharnhorst* and *Gneisnau*, commanded by Rear Admiral Graf von Spee. Either of these German ships could blast Craddock and his cruisers to eternity without coming into the range of the English guns.

It was part of the German Admiralty's design to separate Craddock's cruisers, then lure them southward for the *Scharnhorst* and *Gneisnau* to pick off at will. This was foreseen by the British Admiralty, which took an ambivalent attitude. On the one hand, they urged him to chase every sign of the commerce raiders, while on the other they wanted him not to split his forces in case he encountered the German battle cruisers, whose whereabouts was a mystery.*

* Graf von Spee's two battle cruisers led Craddock into battle on November 1, 1914, at Coronel. The *Good Hope* and the *Monmouth* were shot to pieces. Craddock and the crews of both British ships were killed. There were no survivors. Two months later a major British battle squadron caught von Spee off the Falkland Islands, sinking his ships and killing von Spee and 95 percent of his crews.

Despite the warning not to split his forces, by early September Craddock knew he was tying down 40 percent of his cruiser strength chasing five German ships. At the time he had every reason to believe that these were far faster and better armed than in fact they were. This belief was substantiated by the considerable success the Germans were having. In this area during the first month of the war they appeared to be behaving with insouciance and scoring not only a distinct naval advantage; they were making diplomatic points as well.

This was the time before the angry denunciations of the floating explosive mine and the U-boat. This period was probably one of the last examples of chivalry. Even the official historians of both countries, who have a natural and understandable bias, concede that, although the Germans captured and sank a disproportionate amount of Allied shipping, not one civilian life was lost. A closer look at the activities of the *Dresden, Karlsruhe, Kronprinz Wilhelm,* and the *Kaiser Wilhelm der Grosse,* until her sinking, is essential to understand the British analysis and their countermeasures.

The *Kaiser Wilhelm der Grosse* slipped out of Germany the day war was declared, rounded the north of Scotland, and headed for the South American trade route, sinking the steam tug *Tubal Cain* on the way, having first taken off the crew and accommodated them herself. On August 15 she encountered the Union Castle liner *Galician,* which, like the *Trafalgar,* was fitted with gun rings so that she could be converted in a hurry. What happened then is best told by the *Galician*'s commander, Captain E. M. Day, in his report to the British Admiralty.

On August 15th, at 2:45 P.M. in lat. 27° 30′ N., long. 18° W., we were overhauled by the German armed cruiser *Kaiser Wilhelm der Grosse,* who signaled, "If you communicate by wireless I will sink you." He then ordered us to lower our aerial and to follow him at full speed. At 3:15 P.M. we were ordered to stop. The cruiser destroyed the wireless, inspected the ship's papers, and mustered and inspected all passengers and crew. At 5:30 P.M. the Germans left the ship, taking with them Lieutenant Deane, first-class passenger, and C. Sheerman (gunner), third-class passenger, also all ship's papers and documents, etc. At 5:40 P.M. we were ordered to precede cruiser at full speed and to steer S. 25° W. (magnetic). At 6 P.M. we received orders to keep all lights extinguished, and to have all effects belonging to passengers and crew ready on deck, to provision all boats, and to have everything in order for leaving the ship at daylight. At 8:30 we were ordered to alter to S. 17° E. (magnetic), on which course we continued until 3:40 August 16th, when we received orders to steer S. 45° W. (magnetic), the cruiser throughout following closely in our wake. At 5 A.M. the cruiser sent the following message: "To Captain Day: I will not destroy your ship on account of the women and children on board—you are dismissed—good-bye." To which the following reply was sent: "To German Captain—Most grateful thanks from passengers and crew—good-bye." Lat. 25° 25' N., long. 17° 20' W. The cruiser then left us at full speed and we turned ship and shaped a course for Tenerife.

A further statement was made by Captain Day in the following terms:

Courses.—The *Kaiser Wilhelm der Grosse* did not approach the *Galician* directly, but at first kept wide of us on a parallel course, flying no colors, and it was only when turning in toward us that she hoisted the German ensign. I then ran up the Red Ensign, and it was at this time the German cruiser threatened to sink me unless I stopped wireless communication. The commander of the cruiser then ordered me to follow him, and ultimately to come alongside on his starboard side.

As will be seen from my report above, after the German officer had taken away my papers, we were ordered to alter our courses from time to time, at a speed of 12 knots, in such a way that we steered three triangular courses, obviously as if the cruiser were looking out for some other vessels, and it was possibly owing to failing in this attempt that he at last dismissed my ship and allowed me to proceed on my voyage.

Tobacco.—Having heard that some of the German boatmen were trying to purchase cigars and cigarettes from our men on the lower deck, I passed along word that there must be no trading with this German ship, and this I believe was also done by the German officer who was then in my cabin. After the mustering of the crew and passengers, and the examination and removal of the ship's papers, I asked the German officer if he would take a cigar, and he laughingly observed, "Yes, we have no cigars left." This I felt to be a convenient opportunity for showing my sense of the courtesy with which this individual officer had treated myself and my ship, and I said to him, "If you will have a few cigars or cigarettes, I shall be very pleased." I then sent a steward to fetch 300 cigars and 1,200 cigarettes, which I asked the officer to accept, and he expressed his thanks for this act of courtesy.

In this connection I may add that, after the German cruiser had left us, I was told by several of my first-class passengers that the men in the German boat did not appear to relish their task, and that when asking for cigarettes and tobacco they said, in what appeared almost a state of trembling anxiety, "We do not want to fight; we have no grudge against your English ships."

Medical Stores.—From casual conversation afterwards with passengers, I learned that some of them had been told by the men in the German boat alongside that the *Kaiser Wilhelm der Grosse* had a crew of about 450 men, very largely R.N.R men, and it is significant of the possibility of a considerable amount of sickness being on board that the German officer in charge of the boat's crew took away all the quinine from the surgery of my ship.

The following day, August 16, the *Kaiser Wilhelm der Grosse* stopped the S.S. *Kaipara*, bound from Montevideo with a cargo of refrigerated meat. The entire crew was taken aboard and the *Kaipara* sunk by gunfire. On the 17th, the liner *Arlanza* of some 15,000 tons was halted. Although she carried mail, diplomatic dispatches, and a general cargo, the *Kaiser Wilhelm der Grosse*, on learning that she had passengers aboard, signaled that she was to throw her radio installation overboard. When this had been done, she closed alongside and through a megaphone announced that she was "dismissed on account of your having women and children aboard." The master of the *Arlanza*, Commander C. E. Down, could not believe his ears and hesitated to get under way again. He was then given the same message twice more and eventually took the hint and made off. Three days later the cargo liner *Nyanga* was stopped, her crew taken aboard the German ship, and then sunk. In all, the *Kaiser Wilhelm der Grosse* stopped eleven ships, captured the crews of three of them, and sent the rest on their way. She sent her prisoners on to the then neutral island of Las Palmas two days before the *Highflyer* blew her out of the water.

The *Kronprinz Wilhelm* had been in New York when war was declared. She had slipped out at once and Admiral Craddock had surprised her being armed by the *Karlsruhe* on August 16. The Germans had escaped, but *Kronprinz Wilhelm* had only had time to take on two four-inch guns, which the *Karlsruhe* had taken out of her own armament. She captured a total of thirteen ships without the loss of a life and released any prisoner who would sign a parole not to take any further part in the war. Those who would not sign were sent into neutral ports. She evaded the Royal Navy throughout her career, eventually voluntarily interning herself at Newport, Rhode Island, when her boilers became too burned out to repair. The secret of the *Kronprinz Wilhelm*'s success was her speed, which could top twenty-three knots, almost as fast as the light cruisers *Dresden* and *Karlsruhe*, which were active off Pernambuco.

During the first month of the war these two had each captured seven allied ships, four of them during the first week of September. The *Dresden* had cheekily let several go free after throwing their cargoes overboard if they were thought to be useful to the British war effort; otherwise she merely destroyed the wireless sets aboard. She had written in the log book of the cargo ship *Hostilius*, "Let go because her destruction did not seem worthwhile."

Word of these successes spread rapidly along the South American waterfronts. As far as the seamen were concerned, the Germans threatened no danger as long as war matériel was not carried. They released prisoners onto neutral ground, were courteous to passengers, and appeared to be able to harass at their ease the ships plying the sea lane from Brazil. This was the diplomatic victory that the Germans were gaining, and it was this that Admiral Craddock had orders to stop.

His first plan was to order all ships bound *into* the Plata to steer a course well to seaward of the usual coastal route. This would leave the inshore waters free for him to sweep. He would know that anything heading south could not be friendly. As his blockading cruisers radioed the names and tracks of the outward-bound ships, he would be able to plot their precise positions. Any strange ship must, in his reckoning, be either the *Dresden, Karlsruhe,* or *Kronprinz Wilhelm*. On September 6, there came an unexpected piece of information. It came unwittingly from the *Berwind*.

The little *Eber*, loaded with those not required aboard the *Cap Trafalgar,* had sailed at 10 A.M. on the morning of

138

September 4. It had been an emotional farewell between one party of men off to fight, the other to certain internment for the duration of the war. The musicians and singers, who were equally split between the two ships, led a chorus of community singing until their voices could no longer carry over the water. Captain Wirth had made one final alteration to his plans. He had taken the three most recalcitrant of the six Spanish firemen from the *Berwind* and put them into the *Eber*, in this way replacing three Germans, who he felt would be better off taking their chances with the *Berwind* than suffering internment in Argentina. His secondary reason was that he wanted to avoid any further incidents between the Spaniards and the *Berwind*'s master, which would have been difficult for Langerhannsz to control.

Wirth himself then took the *Cap Trafalgar* out on her first patrol, leaving Langerhannsz in charge of the island and the remaining ships. It was an appointment that had not been well received by the *Berwind*. When Langerhannsz tried to order the *Berwind* to start transferring her coal to the *Pontos* and *Eleonore Wouvermans*, the *Berwind* refused, and from then on her master and crew stayed aloof from the other members of the little garrison. On September 5, the *Berwind*, without seeking permission, radioed her owners in New York. As she did not have them, she did not use German naval codes. She did, however, use a standard American commercial code, coupled to the *Eber*'s old call sign. Her message, which was an attempt to have Wirth's orders overridden, was intercepted and immediately passed to Craddock, who was controlling the sweep of the Plata trade route from his flagship *Good Hope*. It read: "Your original instructions countermanded by local commander. New ordered stay until *Dresden* and *Kronprinz Wilhelm* join *Cap Trafalgar* either here or Rocas. Advise which orders acceptable. *Berwind*."

There was one slight corruption in this message. "Rocas,"

which was the minute island that Wirth was about to inspect and Barr to avoid, was corrupted to "Rocks."

British Naval Intelligence regarded the message as a windfall. They made a series of logical assumptions. First, they assumed the *Eber* was still off the African coast. Second, the mention of the *Cap Trafalgar* confirmed their opinion that the *Cap Trafalgar* had escaped to Africa. The mention of the *Dresden* and *Kronprinz Wilhelm* seemed to imply that Craddock's pressure had succeeded and that Germany was switching her attack to the sea route from South Africa. So now they searched for an area that could be identified as "Rocks."

They found just such a place, called St. Paul's Rocks, 1,500 miles east southeast of the West Indies, just south of the Cape Verde basin, an area where they knew the *Dresden* and *Karlsruhe* had operated before. Here they reasoned was the source of their supplies. Here was the rendezvous where they could catch the entire German raiding flotilla unaware. Of course, the fact that it was not in naval code could be a trap, but it was equally likely that the *Eber*, tin tub of a gunboat that she was, did not have the latest codes. It was a risk the British had to take. Characteristically, they left the decision as to whether or not to take it to Admiral Craddock. He was a brave and honorable man who did not think twice. It could be said that he never thought twice. Without delay, he raced off in *Good Hope* on a fifteen-hundred-mile wild-goose chase, leaving the cruisers *Berwick* and *Bristol* as the only British ships stationed south of the *Cornwall.*

By this time, the British Admiralty had also discovered what armament the *Cap Trafalgar* was meant to have aboard. They found that this was eight of the latest 4.1-inch quick-firing guns, which had a slightly longer range than the 4.7-inch gun that was the standard fitting on British auxiliary cruisers. The *Dresden* mounted twelve 4.1-inchers. So did the *Karlsruhe*, which now had only ten as she had given two away to the *Kronprinz Wilhelm*. However, the British Admiralty was not to know that the *Karlsruhe* had reduced her own to help her consort, or that the *Cap Trafalgar* had only the *Eber*'s antiquated guns. Naval battles and naval tactics were dictated by firepower, by the simple factors of range and weight of shot. The *Kronprinz Wilhelm* was meant to have a further eight, so the tacticians in Whitehall estimated that they were up against a combined firepower of forty guns, each of which could outrange their own 4.7-inchers and would need at least a similar number of 6-inch guns to deal with them. It became vital that the German ships be found and sunk before they grouped together. Once they did so each lookout in the crow's nest could observe a thirty-mile circle of horizon. This would enable them jointly to scout a vast area of ocean and if one sighted an enemy ship, then they could all, because of their superior speed, disperse and reform somewhere else.

Barr and Grant were quite unaware of all this. The somewhat childish contretemps over the challenge to the *Cornwall* had brought their mutual resentment of each other into the open. Each man was both obstinate and proud. Each nursed his own rancor, each took his meals alone, Barr in the chart house, Grant in his, or rather Barr's, old cabin. Their sense of failure somehow permeated the wardroom, where Dr. Maynard, worried by Grant's condition and now by the effect the long hours in the chart house were having on Barr, spent his time trying not only to minister to their medical needs but to effect what could be seen as at least a public reconciliation.

He saw and spoke to Grant, but never broke his patient's confidence, beyond noting that Grant complained that the humidity was affecting his asthma and that he felt he was also developing arthritis. Maynard prescribed rest; there was little else he could do. As the *Carmania* drew further off the land, she escaped the warm currents that flow along the Brazilian coast, and gradually the humidity eased. Grant took Maynard's advice. As the *Carmania* ploughed her solitary way southward, she seemed to have reverted to the passenger liner she really was. Awnings were rigged. The men played deck quoits and other cruise-ship games with equipment they found aboard. Chief Gunner Henry Middleton had the time of his life taking photographs, while Captain Noel Grant took a leisurely convalescence comfortably ensconced in a deck chair.

﹥9﹤

One hundred miles to the east of the *Carmania,* the two colliers *Prussia* and *Ebenberg* steered a parallel course to her as they steamed at a modest ten knots toward Trinidad Island. One hundred miles farther east of the colliers, the *Cap Trafalgar,* making twelve knots, headed for the same rendezvous. The Germans maintained a strict radio silence, but they all heard the *Carmania* every six hours as she reported her position, and as regularly the *Cornwall* and *Bristol* acknowledged her signals. When they did so, they informed the *Carmania* what other friendly ships she might expect to sight, together with details of the courses they were taking. The messages, which naturally were in code, were sometimes both long and complicated. The radio operators frequently asked for "repeats" of doubtful groups of code letters and figures. To the British operators it was a chore; to the listening Germans it was a threat.

To the collier masters and to Captain Wirth, it seemed as if a substantial section of the Royal Navy was just over the horizon. This was understandable as much of the messages was taken up with ships' names, which were rarely encoded. Wirth logged that he identified the *Bristol, Cornwall, Berwick,* and *Monmouth* among others. The latter two were not in the area but may well have been mentioned as the *Cornwall,* the most northerly of the cruisers off Brazil, relayed information back to the remainder of Craddock's squadron scattered between Pernambuco and the West Indies.

Wirth was busy. The more he learned about his ship, the more apprehensive he was. With a funnel unshipped and one condenser partly closed down his maximum speed was 16½ knots, far slower than any British cruiser and slower than many of the merchant ships and auxiliary cruisers he was likely to meet. The *Dresden*, for example, could manage nearly 30 when pushed hard. This meant that if he was ever to get close enough to an enemy, then he was going to have to rely more than ever on his disguise. He tried to keep his misgivings to himself, but among his officers there were no illusions. Feddersen, writing a letter home, wrote, "We know our prospects for success are slim." Lieutenant Klevitz was even blunter. He wrote, "If we meet the enemy, then we haven't a chance."

Whatever their misgivings, Wirth and his officers worked the crew hard. Each day was taken up with battle practice. Fire parties were allocated to different parts of the ship, for fire was their greatest hazard. Although the carpets and curtains had been removed, the ship was a mass of woodwork and paneling, which once on fire would be almost impossible to put out, as the flames could race up the ventilation shafts and break out elsewhere. Every bathtub was filled with water, the hoses were left permanently run out, while every hour decks and sun awnings were hosed down with sea water.

The fire parties were drawn mainly from the cooks and stewards who had remained on board. Each had his own area of responsibility and knew that because of the shortage of crew there would be no one to assist them. Fritz Zirchelbach, the peacetime sauce chef, took charge of the fire parties with his hors d'oeuvre chef Carl Sommer as his second in command.

144

The *Cap Trafalgar* had neither magazines in which to store ammunition nor hoists or trolleys to lift or carry it from the holds. Wirth put men to work to open up the deck hatches. Below each he built a platform about six feet below deck level. On these the ammunition was stacked, and each gun crew was allocated a party of carriers who would bring a steady supply to the gun crews as it was needed. The ammunition parties were led and drilled by Third Officer Schreiner, who had been recruited in Montevideo.

The shells for the two main guns were packed in containers of four. Each shell had to be fitted with a simple impact fuse before it was loaded into the gun. The plan was for someone with nimble fingers to insert the fuses just before the shells were taken over to the guns.

The machine-gun ammunition was loaded in clips, each containing eleven rounds. Each gun had three clips, but the ammunition obtained from the *Dresden* was packed in bulk. This meant that as a clip was emptied in the gun it would have to be taken to the hatch, and dextrous fingers would have to recharge them. Fusing shells, recharging clips, and delivering to the guns was practiced until feet and fingers ached. The timetable upon which Wirth's plan depended allowed only about three minutes between the machine guns coming within range and the boarding parties going over the side. In this period, and under somewhat hazardous circumstances, the machine guns would have to be reloaded as many times as possible. It meant constant practice, though the guns themselves could not be fired, as there was too little ammunition to spare.

Wirth's main preoccupation was the actual boarding operation. As a cadet on the schoolship *Stosch* in 1893, he had practiced boarding, but always from boats the size of one of the *Cap Trafalgar*'s lifeboats. It had been a cheerful competitive pastime, which had usually resulted in an involuntary

,swim for all concerned as rival squads of cadets had struggled their way aboard one or another's longboats. Launching a squad of armed men over the side of the *Cap Trafalgar* was quite a different matter.

To begin with, the *Cap Trafalgar* stood immensely high out of the water. From the rails to the sea was a drop of some forty-five feet. One thing was certain. There was certainly no ship afloat likely to have a higher freeboard. His parties would go either across or down, more likely the latter. The first problem was how far down, the second, how to get down. Remembering Langerhannsz's advice, he went to the library.

Nelson's techniques of grappling irons and boarding ladders, of storming in through the great windows of the stern cabins of French or Spanish four deckers were not applicable. On one occasion, Nelson had run his bowsprit over an enemy's deck and his boarders had swarmed across this. Wirth toyed with the idea of a ramp that perhaps his forward cargo derrick could swing across to a ship alongside, but a few minutes' work with paper and pencil showed this as impractical. In the end he devised two methods that seemed fairly sensible on paper.

The *Cap Trafalgar* carried a great many cargo nets. In these, the cargo and baggage could be slung and the cargo hoists could lift them in and out of the holds. A rough platform was built, laid over an extended net. This was then gathered up at the edges, which were led to a ring into which the hook of the hoist could be inserted. When raised in the air, the contraption looked somewhat similar to a purse or seine such as those used by many coastal fishermen in the Mediterranean. The first boarding party learned to cling to the outside of the net, and Wirth found that he could hoist his party out of the hold, over the side, and down to the estimated deck level of an enemy in just under a minute. The hoist, which could carry three tons, coped adequately with a first wave of thirty boarders. As the *Cap Trafalgar* steamed south, any observer might well have believed he was imagining things as the boarding crew practiced being hoisted out of the hold, across the deck, then lowered until they hovered over the wave tops.

The key man in this part of the operation was the winch operator. The *Cap Trafalgar*'s winches were totally exposed on the foredeck. There was no shelter, even from the weather, for they were designed only for use in port. The first priority was to erect a relatively bulletproof screen, which was made from hatch covers, spare timber, and other materials on board. The second problem was that normally the winch operator depended on signals to tell him when his load was on the quayside, for his view was obstructed by the side of the ship. The signals usually came from either the bridge or a man perched up the foremast. Under battle conditions this would be impracticable, so it was agreed that the operator, once the load was swung well out, would lower away at the speed a man would travel if he had jumped. This maximum lowering speed was learned by lowering the party back into the hold while the winch operator kept his back to them. It was agreed that the signal to send the boarding party across would be the actual impact as the *Cap Trafalgar* ground alongside.

As a failsafe arrangement, and for a secondary party, Wirth had the great carpets brought up on deck. These were lashed to spars which projected over the side, which in turn were secured to the side rails forward of the bridge, so that if certain of the lashings were cut the carpets would unroll downward onto the deck of the ship below. Between the supporting spars, a rough and ready platform was made so access could be gained to the carpets, which were planned to be used as a chute.

The two boarding parties had separate battle stations. The first were to group in the forehold, the second to lie flat on the floor of the second-class dining room, which led directly out onto the foredeck. Both numbered thirty men. The first or hold party were all regular *Eber* seamen, equipped with rifles and bayonets. The second wave was a scratch crew of stokers and engine-room hands, who had to rummage for whatever weapon they could find among their tools. Wirth reckoned that, once he was alongside, there would be no further need for his stokers until the matter had been decided one way or another.

As an added refinement, and to obscure an opponent's view as to what was happening, he had steam hoses rigged so that, as the ships touched, a series of jets of steam could be turned on the foredeck and bridge of his enemy.

The boarders' instructions were simple. They were to reach the bridge of whatever ship they attacked, take it over, and signal the engine room to stop engines. They were then and only then to attempt to silence her armament. When this had been achieved, all stairs and hatches leading below deck were to be sealed and guarded. By this time, if not before, his prey would have struck her flag. He placed Lieutenant Klevitz in charge of the "hold party," and Feddersen in charge of the "carpet party."

The novelty of the operation appealed to everyone aboard, with the exception of Dr. Ludwig Violet, the *Eber*'s surgeon. He noted in his diary, "I devoutly hope we do not take part in any action under any circumstances."

The other officers were more sanguine. Feddersen and his "carpet party" were dubbed "Ali Baba and his thirty thieves."

As the *Cap Trafalgar* drew nearer to the island, the British wireless traffic appeared to increase and become louder. On the evening of September 12, Wirth decided that it would be courting disaster to continue to use Trinidad any more. He sent out a previously agreed coded message to Langerhannsz via the *Berwind*'s radio. Only Langerhannsz would know that it read that he must be ready to evacuate the island within twenty-four hours.

Commander Langerhannsz had watched the *Cap Trafalgar* sail away on her patrol with mixed feelings. He half expected not to see her again. That concerned him, both for the sake of his ship and the men aboard her. On the other hand the stress and excitement of the last three weeks had taken their toll. First he felt relieved, then lonely. With the *Cap Trafalgar* gone, the little anchorage seemed more than empty. It seemed desolate. He missed the size and spaciousness of his ship. The *Eleonore Wouvermans,* no matter how pleasant Captain Collmorgen, her master, tried to be to him, was as uncomfortable and as dirty as only an aged collier in tropical waters could be. The *Pontos* had come alongside and was busy transferring her cargo, while the master of the *Berwind* remained with his ship, ignoring both his consorts and his orders. In an effort to escape his depression, Langerhannsz decided to go explore. If he was to be in command, then, he decided, he should see exactly what his command consisted of. Taking his shotgun, he had himself rowed ashore.

There were the remains of a jetty with a ramshackle stone building at one end. From this, smoke curled lazily upward, and there was the sound of activity within. All around were thickets of rough thorn with the signs of a path that had been hacked through them, which presumably led to the lookout point high on the hill above. Langerhannsz noticed that the southwest of the island was luxurious with thorn thickets and a few low trees. Higher up it turned to rock, with tufts of grass and thorn growing sparsely in crevices and hollows. The hilltop shimmered in the heat, so Langerhannsz chose to explore the building first.

Inside he found Dr. Braunholz, who had been placed in charge of the livestock that the *Eber, Steiemark,* and *Cap*

Trafalgar had brought with them. The egregious little doctor had made himself very comfortable. There were a makeshift bed, a table, a cheerful fireplace with several cooking utensils, which Langerhannsz recognized as coming from the *Cap Trafalgar*, as did the crockery, the cutlery, and almost certainly the several boxes of cigars and crates of wine that were stacked at one end. Braunholz's books were stacked by the bed, and the doctor himself was stirring something on the fire. He was just preparing his luncheon, he told his visitor, and invited him to stay and eat with him. Putting his shotgun against the wall, Langerhannsz accepted the invitation.

Braunholz was supremely happy. He had not even noticed that the *Cap Trafalgar* had left. He had, he explained, been out reading his instruments. He told Langerhannsz that he had unpacked some of his equipment, and was busy recording the temperature and the rainfall. Although he had only been there a week, he was quite sure that the climate was ideal— perfect for pig breeding.

Langerhannsz dutifully inquired after the pigs. They were thriving. Inspired by the *Cap Trafalgar*, Braunholz had christened them Nelson and Emma. Emma apparently was not only in pig—but due to add to the island's population at any moment. His main problem was to clear a space in order to grow food for them. Nelson was happily rooting about in the thickets, but there was some decent soil on this side of the island. Possibly, Braunholz thought, it might grow yams, or some tuberous root vegetable. Perhaps next time a supply ship went to the mainland they could buy some seed. It could be ordered by radio, could it not? Langerhannsz, reflecting that it would be a crime to intrude on Braunholz's dream, agreed that indeed it could be radioed for. He would speak to Captain Wirth on his return.

Finishing his lunch and helping himself to one of the *Cap Trafalgar*'s cigars, Langerhannsz took up his shotgun and set

150

off to walk up to the observation post. The *Eber*'s chickens scratched busily in the dust, while the birds from the Winter Garden sat patiently around the thickets, wondering at their newfound freedom. The climb was a long one, almost a mile, and in parts the track was overgrown. As he picked his way, Langerhannsz noticed what looked very much like a piece of railway line. Scrabbling in the grass, he found the remains of what had obviously been a primitive miniature railway, such as might be found in a quarry or coal mine. It was rusty and no longer usable, but by following the line of the track, he found a much easier way to the summit, though it took longer, for it curved around the hill.

The view was magnificent. He calculated the hilltop stood some five hundred feet above sea level and gave a clear view in all directions for at least twenty miles. The horizon was clear, and the men in the observation post seemed well organized and alert. They had made their bivouac in what appeared to be the remains of some old stone fortifications. Those not on duty were picking around the ruins, shouting cheerfully as they found some souvenir of previous visitors to the island.

Trinidad had been known to seamen since the seventeenth century. The first visitors had been Spaniards, who had found it a handy refuge with a safe anchorage and ample fresh water, and more importantly, a useful reference point for navigation. The Spaniards had garrisoned it from time to time, and since the collapse of Spanish sea power, there had been a variety of settlements.

This was the island that Barr had last visited in 1884, where, in the nineteenth century, a group of Protestant Scots settlers, scared off from Argentina by religious antagonism, had attempted to start a colony, which they planned to support by growing the castor-oil plant. As South America became more stable, and castor oil became cheaper to produce elsewhere, the settlement had been abandoned. The main visitors since then had been seamen, anxious to avoid exorbitant harbor charges and the badly charted hazards of the eastern South American coast. They used Trinidad for the same purpose as had the Spaniards centuries earlier, for fresh water and as a navigational datum point, before they attempted the eastward crossing of the Atlantic.

Leading down from the summit was a different track from the one he had come up. It appeared to run along a ridge that ended in a steep cliff overhanging the sea. The top of the cliff was densely overgrown and over the trees a flock of birds circled. Thinking that they might be worth a shot or two for the pot, he headed toward them. The track broadened out as he entered the trees. They were a type of Scots pine, their trunks bent and twisted by the wind. Underfoot was a thick carpet of pine needles, and beneath these he realized there was a paved path, which began to slope toward the cliff edge. He followed it, and came into what he recognized instantly as a fortification or old-fashioned gun embrasure. There could be no doubt about what its use might have been, for it was still in use. Squatting menacingly behind a low parapet looking directly over the sea below was a gun.

It was not a gun in the modern sense of the word. It was what is known today as a mortar or siege mortar. The diameter of the bell-shaped muzzle was approximately fifty centimeters, while the length of the short stubby barrel was no more than a meter. At the inside base of the barrel was a smaller powder chamber, which was pierced by a touch hole on one side. It appeared to be made of bronze and was mounted on a timber carriage, which was strengthened by several bands of iron. Langerhannsz's academic eyes divined that the carriage was of a later period than the barrel, but a rough metal quadrant fitted to one side of the carriage and calibrated with the angles to which the barrel could be tilted was obviously original to the gun. Beside the carriage stood a small pile of round iron shot.

Peering over the edge of the embrasure, he saw that, if the gun was fired, it would be possible to drop the shot straight through the decks of ships anchored below. Mentally he tried to visualize the effect of a ball, weighing he judged about 45 pounds, if it crashed down on the deck of the *Cap Trafalgar*. It would, he calculated, have a velocity of around 140 miles an hour and would probably go straight through the ship. As he hurried back to the anchorage, his mind was busy, calculating the amount of powder needed to put a 45-pound ball into its maximum trajectory, what the range would be, in what useful way it could be employed. Nelson had both used them and been up against such a weapon at Malta. That was where he had lost his eye, when one of those vast pieces of shot had sent a shower of splinters. But then the French had used stone shot, quarried from beneath Valletta. The Spaniards had used metal shot, which they had heated until it was red hot, and he had read that some English men-of-war used them to clear the decks of boarders or mutinous crews. By the time he had reached the *Eleonore Wouvermans*, he had the outline of a plan in his mind.

To begin with, he would have the barrel dismounted from its carriage and manhandled down to the jetty. If it had been taken up there, then it could come down. It was simply a question of sweat. He supposed it weighed about four hundred pounds. He would have to build another carriage and have the engineers make some sockets for the swivel pins to rest on. By Braunholz's shack there were a few of the railway ties he had acquired in Buenos Aires, which had been used to float ashore some of the heavier stores, such as drums of oil.

The old cannon balls seemed to have rusted together. They

would have to be checked. If they were unusable, it should not be too difficult to devise a projectile, but why only use it as a mortar? If it was filled with, say, coal chips well soaked in oil, it would blast a hail of glowing coals across the deck of any ship the *Cap Trafalgar* tried to board. They in turn would start fires, cause a smokescreen, confusion, surprise.

The *Cap Trafalgar* had gangway ports let into her sides below the bridge so passengers embarking came straight from the passenger terminal onto B deck. If the mortar was set behind those, it would be the same as opening gun ports and blasting a hole in the enemy's side. It was an intoxicating vision.

Fritz Langerhannsz was essentially a peaceful man. His first reaction to the news that his country was at war had been one of distaste. He had viewed the excitability of the attaché in Buenos Aires with ill-concealed annoyance, and the long and furtive trip to the island had been done more from the sense of challenge to his seamanship and a desire to protect his ship than from martial ardor. Julius Wirth he had helped out of compassion and because it was his duty. Nevertheless the sight of the old bronze mortar, probably Spanish, he thought, had done something to his personal chemistry. It had awakened an echo of something that had probably been planted in his mind during his vast reading of naval history. There was nothing of the pirate in Commander Langerhannsz. He was a gentleman, but the thought processes that an abandoned Spanish siege weapon generated were those of a very bloodthirsty gentleman indeed.

When he broached his ideas to Captain Collmorgen, who commanded the *Eleonore Wouvermans*, he was delighted to find him cooperative. Collmorgen had not the slightest objection to having whatever infernal machine he liked mounted on his forecastle. Langerhannsz had no intention of firing it there, it was simply the highest part of the ship that he could put alongside the *Cap Trafalgar* when she returned. It is unlikely Collmorgen would have minded if he had fired it. He had a tremendous admiration for Langerhannsz and dined out for years afterward on his recollections of their service together. While the crews of both ships sweated to transfer the coal, the *Eleonore Wouvermans'* engineer took a party up to the hilltop to bring the mortar down. It was simpler than anyone thought it could be. The *Pontos* had a great number of old rubber tires draped around her sides to protect her plates when coaling from ship to ship. These were sent for, the barrel inserted through the tires like an axle, and using ropes and the brawn of his stokers as brakes, the engineer rolled the mortar down to the quay. Still wrapped in the tires, it was then secured to three empty oil drums, floated out to the collier, and hoisted aboard.

A stout platform and carriage were rigged on the forecastle out of railway ties; swivel sockets were beaten out of strip iron and bolted into position. While this was being done, the engineers inspected the casting for faults or flaws and pronounced it sound. The only problem was that the pile of iron shot was hopelessly annealed together with rust. It was unusable as projectiles. This proved easily surmountable. They took precise measurements of the diameter of the bore and using these cast their own shot, using scrap metal from the engine room set into a cast of lead. When the lead cooled, the final projectiles were found to be slightly too small. Langerhannsz remembered a trick he had read about when the first smooth-bore cannon had been used to fire cannister as opposed to round shot. The outside of his home-made ammunition was bound with tarred rope, which made an effective seal and it was hoped would glow from the heat of the explosion when the mortar was fired. Should it hit its target, it was likely to start a fire.

By the time he received Captain Wirth's message to be

prepared to evacuate the base, the mortar was mounted proudly on the forecastle, and beside it stood three solid projectiles and a variety of containers full of the best Welsh anthracite steeped in oil.

Second Officer Bunte made an uncomfortable passage to Bahía. He arrived off the coast on the evening of September 11, and true to his orders hove to about five miles offshore, determined to ride out the swell until the 13th. There was plenty of shipping about, but he was pleased to note that at first he was ignored. The *Eber* looked like a man-of-war, albeit a very small one, but she flew no flag, as Captain Wirth had taken her ensign. When eventually he was challenged, by a passing pilot boat, Bunte hoisted the signal that he was in quarantine, hoping to gain a few hours' delay. At noon on Saturday, September 12, the pilot boat came out to him again and ordered him to come in and anchor in the outer harbor. No one came out to the ship until Tuesday, the 15th, and Bunte believed he had done his duty as instructed.

The *Eber* had, however, come to the notice of the British Consulate. An unknown official had noted the name and, as a matter of course, telegraphed the British Legation in Buenos Aires. The effect was electric. If circumstances and coincidence had laid the powder train, it was that anonymous official's telegram that lit the fuse. Buenos Aires telegraphed Montevideo, which radioed to the *Bristol*, which relayed to the *Cornwall*, which in turn passed the message back to naval headquarters in the West Indies. The *Eber*'s presence destroyed the whole of the logical assumptions on which Craddock's dash to St. Paul's Rocks had been based. The *Eber* had been going to rendezvous with the *Dresden*, *Kronprinz Wilhelm*, and *Cap Trafalgar*. That had only been a week ago, and now for at least twenty-four hours she had been lying off

Bahía with God knows what disease aboard. That meant that the rendezvous was within five—possibly six—days' steaming of Bahía. The *Eber* had a maximum speed of 14 knots on paper, more likely around 12 after a trip across the Atlantic, say 280 miles a day—1,400 miles. A quick circle drawn on the map passed right through the Vas Rocks to the east of Trinidad Island.

Once more the Admiralty radio network hummed. Once more the operators on the *Cap Trafalgar,* still out on her first patrol, monitored the unknown ciphers. They logged the names *Bristol* and *Cornwall,* then they logged the name of the *Eber.*

ɔ10ɕ

Wirth's first reaction had been to assume that the *Eber* was lost. He knew that Bunte would have scuttled his ship if he had been challenged, so either that was what had happened or some British cruiser had blasted her out of the water without asking questions. Inwardly, he mourned for his ship and its crew. Outwardly, he merely increased speed and redoubled the crew's battle practice. Trinidad was sighted at noon on September 13, and after a wary scout around the island to ensure that the British had not arrived before him, he dropped anchor close to the *Eleonore Wouvermans* shortly after 5 P.M. The latest messages that he had intercepted indicated that there were two British ships quite close to him. He judged the strongest signal to be not more than a hundred miles away.

The *Carmania* received her orders to inspect the Vas Rocks and Trinidad Island at 10 A.M. on the 13th. She altered her heading to take her on a course that would pass directly between the two islands, approaching them from the north. As she did not wish to arrive in the area during darkness, she reduced speed so that the islands would be sighted early in the morning of the 14th.

The approach was chosen after she received the briefing of the ships that she might come across. They were, with the exception of the French sailing barque *Châteaubriand,* all

German: the *Dresden, Kronprinz Wilhelm,* and the *Cap Trafalgar,* which might or might not be accompanied by colliers. The instructions specifically stressed that their mission was to be one of inspection. They were to see, without being seen, for the great height of her topmast gave her, at least in the minds of those who drafted her orders, a distinct advantage. She was merely to show her topmast over the horizon, and make a closer inspection only if there was no sign of the enemy. If there were enemy ships in the area, she was to radio the *Bristol,* which, meanwhile, was taking up a station midway between Trinidad and the coast.

The messages had a pronounced effect on both Grant and Barr. Grant was still obeying Maynard's orders and taking life very gently. However, they had barely decoded before he was in the chart house discussing courses and tactics with Barr. He asked Barr to describe the islands they had been ordered to inspect. He learned of the anchorage and the fresh-water spring in the southwest part of Trinidad. It was for that reason that he decided to approach from the north, and it was at that moment that Barr realized that Grant wished to have the island between himself and whatever ships might be anchored there. Obviously he had decided to ignore his orders. If they were to be obeyed to the letter, then Grant should have set his course so that he could view the island from his highest lookout post from the southwestern horizon and thereby obtain an unimpeded view.

Soon the two men were deep in studying the silhouettes of the German ships they might expect to discover. The *Dresden* was a low, rangy light cruiser with four funnels, a reputed speed of 24 knots or more, displacing a modest 4,500 tons. The *Kronprinz Wilhelm* was a four-funneled liner, capable of 23 knots, while the *Cap Trafalgar* was, like the *Carmania,* a triple-screwed turbine liner, approximately their own size and equipped with three funnels. She had a designed speed of 18 knots, one knot faster than themselves. The same thought went through both men's minds at the same time. If the Germans could be led into thinking that they were the *Cap Trafalgar,* then the *Dresden, Kronprinz Wilhelm,* and the colliers might allow them to get within range. It did not occur to either of them to dwell on what might happen if the *Cap Trafalgar* was anchored there. They perhaps assumed that she would mistake them for one of the many three-funneled German and Italian liners that worked the Atlantic during peacetime.

The remainder of the day was spent knocking up a dummy third funnel. It was a simple structure made from deck awnings stretched over a light timber frame. The frame was in the shape of a V with the point on the forward side, as they were interested only in showing a three-funneled silhouette when viewed either from the front or a quarter profile. The frame was secured behind their second or what was now their center funnel, and held in position by cables. This fresh activity was welcomed by Maynard, who shortly afterward had the opportunity to ensure that Grant and Barr cemented their re-established relationship.

The coolness between them had developed into a coolness between Grant and the regular Navy officers on the one side, and the Cunarders on the other. The camaraderie that Grant had been at pains to inspire at Bermuda had evaporated. Now it was only the thought of an action the following day that held the unsettled officers together. It was Maynard's dread that their mission would turn out to be a wild-goose chase, and that in the frustration and disappointment that would follow a much more serious situation might develop.

September 13 was a Sunday. Toward evening Grant was conducting ship's prayers on the stern deck when a signaler brought a message to Lieutenant Murchie, the duty officer on the bridge. He opened and read it. It was a brief message from

Captain Ellerman of the H.M.S. *Cornwall,* stating that Head-quarters West Indies Station had pleasure in relaying birthday greetings from Mrs. Grant and that he and his officers aboard the *Cornwall* "associated themselves with that good lady's sentiment." Murchie had the cable placed in Grant's cabin, but the message and the fact that their supposedly bachelor captain had a wife were known to every officer on the ship within minutes.

Maynard believed it provided the perfect excuse for the safety valve. A brief consultation with Barr, the other officers, and then with the chefs resulted in an invitation to Grant on behalf of Commander Barr and the members of the wardroom requesting the pleasure of his company for dinner in the wardroom that evening. Grant accepted with pleasure.

That Sunday morning was a busy one for Langerhannsz. The *Berwind* still had her coal aboard. The *Pontos* was empty, and the *Eleonore Wouvermans's* bunkers were now nearly full. As the *Berwind*'s captain was still being recalcitrant, there was no coaling to do. The time was spent preparing to evacuate the island. The stores that had been landed were taken further into the thickets and hidden away from prying eyes. Most of the livestock was collected and crated, but Dr. Braunholz resolutely refused to leave. As far as he was concerned, the German Navy was welcome to the scrofulous African pigs that had been shipped on the *Steiemark,* but it was quite impossible to move Emma. She was due to pig at any moment. Wearily Langerhannsz compromised, and agreed to leave Braunholz, with an ample supply of food, in charge of the stores that had been hidden on the island. He also gave him a signed certificate stating that he was a German citizen, was exempt from military service, and had played no part in hostilities. Lastly he promised him he would inform the German consulate in Montevideo that he was there, so that he would not be forgotten. "Remind him about the seed," said the doctor.

The lookouts reported the *Cap Trafalgar* on the horizon at noon. When she eventually steamed into the anchorage, Langerhannsz was on his hands and knees beside his mortar, trying to calibrate the quadrant scale with the scale of his own sextant. He had hardly had sufficient time to clean himself up when Wirth summoned all officers to a conference aboard the *Cap Trafalgar*.

Wirth explained that the *Eber* was probably lost, that the British radio signals were getting closer by the hour, and that it was time for them all to slip away to the south and establish a new base in some secluded bay on the coast of southern Argentina. Langerhannsz confirmed that the *Pontos* and *Eleonore Wouvermans* were ready to sail, but that the *Berwind* was still loaded. He suggested that, rather than accompany them, it might be better for the *Pontos* to return to collect another cargo from Montevideo, unless of course the *Berwind* would transfer her cargo.

The *Berwind*'s master was adamant. He had orders to transfer his coal to the *Cap Trafalgar* and no one else. As it was dangerous to his ship to do so, then he would return with his coal aboard. He would not under any circumstances hand the coal over to a third party. He would never, he said, be able to obtain payment for it from the Admiralty if he did. When orders said, "Supply *Cap Trafalgar,*" they meant the *Cap Trafalgar* and that was that.

Wirth realized that he was up against a stupid and bureaucratic, as opposed to a villainous, mind. He suggested a compromise. He would give the *Berwind* a receipt from the *Cap Trafalgar* for her coal, and the *Berwind* could load it onto the *Pontos* as soon as they arrived at the new rendezvous. "Impossible," the *Berwind*'s master replied. He had been ordered to Trinidad Island and nowhere else. The master of the *Berwind* now agreed to transfer the coal to the *Pontos* in exchange for a receipt from the *Cap Trafalgar*, but only if it was done at Trinidad Island. Wirth conceded the point. He desperately needed the coal and with all hands it should not take long to shift. However, it was now too late in the evening to start the transfer, and because of the proximity of the British cruisers, he dared not work by floodlight.

He ordered that work should start at dawn, which was around 4 A.M. By then, he told Captain Collmorgen, he wanted him to have the *Eleonore Wouvermans* positioned on the southwest horizon to keep a sharp lookout for the British. Should they see a mast, Collmorgen was to signal him and it was hoped this would give everyone time to scatter. If they had to do so, he advised them all to make for neutral harbors and report to the nearest German consul, who would advise them in due course of the next rendezvous.

Collmorgen asked how he was to signal, as he had no radio. He could, of course, try with his heliograph to the lookouts on the hill, or perhaps he should fire Langerhannsz's infernal machine. It was the first Wirth had heard of this, and he listened incredulously as Langerhannsz explained his ideas to him. He was told that it had been designed for the *Cap Trafalgar*, and his heart warmed to the old captain as he explained the variations of use he had devised. Wirth had no wish to hurt the older man's feelings and gently suggested that, for the time being, the mortar stay on Collmorgen's ship, where in the last resort it would be useful as a signal— preferably with a charge of coal dust. Langerhannsz asked if he could have some black blasting powder with which to load it. He had none himself, and he knew there was plenty on the *Cap Trafalgar*, where it was used for "fog maroons," rescue rocket equipment, and other uses such as propelling flares into the sky during a night-time emergency. Wirth told him to help himself.

As he closed the meeting, he invited all those present to attend an evening service that he had arranged for 7:30 that evening. They would be welcome to bring those members of their crews who could be spared and wished to attend.

The birthday party was an unqualified success. The kitchens, drawing on the *Carmania*'s enormous range of delicacies and well-stocked wine cellar, produced a meal that for quality of cooking and range of courses probably would have compared well with such other premartial occasions as the Duchess of Richmond's ball on the eve of Waterloo. The dinner was followed by a recital by the ship's band, and the combined aromas of Havana, Mouton Rothschild, and fine cognac lingered until the following day. Barr had his moment of triumph when he proposed the toast to the ladies. After it had been drunk, he called for the glasses to be refilled and, with the officers still standing, he called for a toast to "one lady in particular, Mrs. Grant." Grant blushed like a schoolboy.

There was some good-natured banter about their attempt to disguise themselves. Edwin Maynard, delighted with the success of his stratagem, called for a toast to the ship, adding that he did not know whether to propose the H.M.S. *Carmania* or the *Cap Trafalgar*. In the present circumstances he would settle for H.M.S. *Sybarite*. Their evening ended with each in turn singing one or another of the rich repertoire of sea songs, with everyone joining in the choruses. Trinidad Island was now only fifty miles to the south.

Julius Wirth had been brought up as a Lutheran. Normally he let his faith sit lightly upon him, but he saw his duty as a ship's captain as including the spiritual well-being of his men. He did not take the attitude that they should be taught to fear God and honor the Kaiser and that would be enough. His faith went deeper than that, as it did and does with so many

164

seamen, particularly those in positions of responsibility. It was his usual practice to hold a weekly service on the *Eber,* but in the helter-skelter of the last few weeks he had omitted them. That Sunday, he wished not only to catch up on what he regarded as his spiritual obligations, he also wished to remember the *Eber* and her crew. He had not mentioned her presumed loss to any except his officers, and the omission weighed upon his conscience. Instead of a brief prayer meeting, he had ordered a full-scale "evensong" and had let it be known that it was his wish that the remaining members of the *Cap Trafalgar*'s orchestra should join with those members of the opera company who shared the stokehold with them, and provide both music and vocal backing to the service.

No record survives as to what hymns were sung or what prayers offered. Dr. Braunholz, sitting beside his shack on the jetty, saw the boats row over from the surrounding colliers, their oars making tiny splashes of phosphorescence in the water. He recalled a great bubble of music, swelled by several hundred voices, rolling up into the hills above him and echoing across the moonlit anchorage. He recalled the long intervals of silence, more music, and then the strains of the National Anthem, which awoke some inner sentiment that compelled him to get to his feet and stand to attention. Then the boats rowed back again to their parent ships, and a total stillness settled over the little gathering of ships. He remembered a deep longing to belong to the company of men across the water and at the same time a profound sense of relief that he did not.

Langerhannsz delayed his departure after the service. He wished to speak to Wirth, and he sensed that Wirth needed someone to talk to. They walked together along the boat deck, past the unfamiliar shapes of the machine guns shrouded in their spray covers, through the Winter Garden and into the library. Apart from the absence of a carpet it appeared much as it always had. On one wall Nelson was portrayed watching the French Fleet burn off the Nile. On another he lay dying on the deck of the *Victory*. Wirth poured two glasses of brandy and remarked, "I must say, at this particular moment I find your choice of pictures in remarkably bad taste."

Langerhannsz remained silent, so Wirth continued. He admitted that he found the strain of being the quarry difficult to stomach. But yet this was the moment that he had trained for. This was the reason for his being in the Navy. He supposed that in some ways he should be glad. Tomorrow would be the eighteenth anniversary of his being commissioned a Leutnant zur See and posted to his first ship, the little panzership *Frithjof und Hildebrande*. He spoke of his career, his parents, and, as Langerhannsz recalled, "the things a man does speak of and which I understood he needed to speak of." When he had finished, he invited Langerhannsz to come with him to the radio cabin.

The operator dozed by the set. Wirth asked him if there had been any recent traffic. On being told that the last British transmission had been about an hour ago, Wirth asked him for his estimate of the distance. The operator thought for a moment and then remarked that it could not have been more than fifty miles.

The news seemed to strengthen Wirth, as though he had taken a long-considered decision and immediately felt the better for it. He took Langerhannsz down to his cabin, unlocked his desk, and produced his war diary and some correspondence. He gave them to him, asking him to look after them for a while. "Come," he said, "I will arrange for a boat to take you over to your ship. Tell Collmorgen I expect to see him and his ship on the watch position at first light." He added, "Whatever you see or hear, do not turn back. We will meet, I have no doubt, in due course." Langerhannsz saluted and went down the gangway to the waiting boat. When it reached the *Eleonore Wouvermans,* Langerhannsz asked the oarsmen to wait for a few moments. He came up with a book, which he asked them to give to the Captain on their return.

It was Volume II of Southey's *Life of Nelson;* a page was neatly marked and some words were underlined. They may have been in bad taste, or they may have comforted. They were what is known today as the "Trafalgar Memorandum," Nelson's final instructions to his captains before Trafalgar. The part Langerhannsz had marked read: "The business of a Commander is first to bring an enemy's fleet to battle on the most advantageous terms to himself (I mean that of laying his ships close on board the enemy) as expeditiously as possible; and secondly to continue them there, without separating, until the business is decided. . . . No Captain can do very wrong if he places his ship alongside that of an enemy."

ꙮ 11 ꙮ

Braunholz rose early and went to check his meteorological
instruments. It was going to be a fine day, the heat tempered
by a stiff northeasterly breeze. Already the ships in the
anchorage were busy. The *Berwind* and the *Pontos* alongside
each other, winches chattering, derricks topped, the familiar
pall of coal dust hanging over them. The *Cap Trafalgar* had
steam up, but her crew were swarming over to the colliers by
the boatload, stripped down to their waists, shovels in their
hands. The *Eleonore Wouvermans* was a distant wisp of smoke
on the southwestern horizon.

Lieutenant Feddersen landed at the jetty with a team of
men, who set about transferring the livestock that had been
brought from Africa. As each animal or fowl was caught and
loaded, he marked it off on a ledger. Feddersen was obviously
taking official regulations about responsibility for property
very seriously. He handed Braunholz a similar ledger, which
contained a complete inventory of the stores that had been left
behind. He told them that he was to check and inspect them
every day and that he must sign his name each time he made
an inspection. Should any ship call and remove any of them, it
was Braunholz's duty to obtain a receipt. He mentioned that
he had brought over some medical supplies for him and asked
him to be so good as to sign for them.

At 9:30, the lookout party came down from the hilltop and boarded Feddersen's boat, which then rowed back to the ship. Braunholz was now alone on the island.

At 10 A.M. he heard Captain Wirth hailing the colliers through his megaphone. They had under an hour to complete their coal transfer. He would sound his whistle at 10:50. They were to sail no later than 11:00.

In the meantime Wirth had sent for Lieutenant Klevitz and the engineering officers. He reminded them that it was a tradition in the German Navy that no ship should ever be captured by the enemy. If there was a risk of that happening, then it was the captain's or the senior surviving officer's duty to scuttle the ship. Wirth gave instructions for explosive charges to be placed along the *Cap Trafalgar*'s keel plates. These were to be exploded only on his order. Lieutenant Klevitz was to test the detonating circuits and report when the charges were in position.

At 10:50 the *Cap Trafalgar*'s whistle sounded. As her crew streamed aboard, Wirth unpacked the battle ensign that the *Dresden* had given him, folded it properly, and attaching it to the signal halyards hoisted it to the crosstrees of the mast. A solitary line led down from the folded flag to the deck. One pull would break the ensign free from its folds, to flutter bravely in the stiff northeasterly breeze.

Langerhannsz knelt beside his mortar on the foredeck of the collier. He had loaded his black powder into small green baize bags in which the *Cap Trafalgar*'s silver was usually kept. He knew that the master gunners of earlier times had preferred linen to keep their powder dry, but he hopefully assumed that baize would do as well. He stuffed the powder chamber with a carefully calculated measure, tamped it down, and added a further wad of baize as a precaution. Next he charged the barrel with a mixture of anthracite steeped in oil, into which he tossed a few handfuls of powder, sealing the mixture in with a further covering of baize. He inserted a length of fuse into a small detonator, crimped it with his teeth, then inserted the detonator into the touch hole, securing it with a few pinches of powder and a screw of cotton waste. The fuse was of a length that would give approximately ten seconds' burning time. It stretched to the top of the jump ladder leading up from the main deck to the foredeck. Checking that he had both matches and cigars in his pocket, he joined Collmorgen on the bridge.

They had decided that if a British cruiser showed its hull on the horizon they would flash a heliograph signal to the *Cap Trafalgar,* and then sail toward the cruiser. They would be stopped for inspection, and by causing a diversion with the mortar they planned to gain Wirth as much time as possible. If a cruiser did stop them, then, as it came alongside, it was due for the surprise of its life.

The lookout on the *Carmania*'s masthead spotted the top of the hill bearing two points on the starboard bow at 9:30 A.M. Grant promptly altered course to south southwest to bring it dead ahead and increased speed to sixteen knots. The island was approximately thirty miles distant. At 10 A.M. the crews were sent to an early meal, and when the whole island came into view at 10:45, the ship went into action stations. Grant and Barr studied the island through their glasses. At 11:04 A.M. they spotted three sets of masts behind the western edge, and as they watched, the taller of the three moved westward to clear the headland. "It looks," said Barr to Grant, "as if we have some company."

ɔ12ɕ

The *Cap Trafalgar* steered a southwesterly course away from the oncoming *Carmania*, which was now some 15,000 yards distant, steering a similar course to her own. Wirth ordered his signaler to warn the *Eleonore Wouvermans,* while the *Pontos* and *Berwind* worked up speed as they followed him. Wirth hoped to lure the strange ship, which must be British, so that when he made his turn to attack, she would have him on one side and the island on the other, thus limiting her ability to maneuver away from him. Together with Feddersen, he climbed up to the top of the bridge and tried to identify who the intruder was.

Feddersen was perplexed. He thought she might be one of theirs, suggesting that she was remarkably like their sister ship *Cap Finisterre.* Calling his signaler, Wirth ordered him to flash a message asking the ship to identify herself.

Grant took one look as the *Cap Trafalgar* cleared the land, exposing her enormous hull and upperworks. "Good God," he turned to Barr beside him. "Who is she?" Barr was flummoxed. "From her funnels, she's one of ours, maybe Union Castle line." Grant ordered a radio message to be transmitted, ordering his quarry to identify herself. At the same time, he ordered the white ensign to be hoisted. They were still about 15,000 yards apart, and still steering the same

171

course. Grant suspected a trap. There might well be yet more ships sheltering behind the island. He altered course slightly to give himself more sea room. Barr was thinking the same and said, "It looks as if he has support behind the land."

"If he does," replied Grant, "we shall soon know."

As the white ensign broke from the *Carmania*'s masthead, Wirth identified it, and seconds later noticed the alteration in course. As he had now worked up his maximum speed, he put his ship into a full 180° turn so that he was now headed directly at the enemy. He called down to the engine room, asked for maximum steam, and warned them to be ready for the violent maneuvers they had practiced with the *Eber*. Standing in the center of his bridge, he squinted down his foredeck, lining up his foremast and his bows at the *Carmania*'s bridge. The *Cap Trafalgar* had lost quite a lot of ground during the turn. The two ships were now no more than 10,000 yards apart.

Commander Lockyer and Midshipman Colson stood in the gun control, peering into the Barr and Stroud rangefinder, Lockyer calling off the range as it decreased. At 12:10 P.M. he called, "In range, sir." Grant leaned over the bridge, and shouted down to Henry Middleton, who stood beside No. 1 gun on the port side.

"Load with solid shot, fire across his bows—don't hit him—fire."

Middleton's shot splashed into the water a hundred yards ahead of the *Cap Trafalgar.* Wirth promptly broke his ensign free, and ordered his two guns to return fire.

They had been told to concentrate on the bridge and upperworks. Wirth wished to capture the ship, its armament, stores, and coal. He did not want a sinking hulk on his hands. His first shot went over the top of the *Carmania;* with the second he managed to bring down her signal halyards and radio mast; the third knocked out one of the *Carmania*'s guns, killing most of the gun crew.

Two shells from the *Carmania* smacked into the Winter Garden. Splinters flew everywhere, piercing the deck steam pipes and starting several small fires. The range was now decreasing every second. Wirth believed that in another two minutes he would be able to use his machine guns. A splinter killed the helmsman behind him. The wheel spun wildly as the man fell, and the *Cap Trafalgar* yawed to her port side, leaving the *Carmania* at an angle of some 30° to her starboard now. Wirth leaped to the wheel himself, using all his strength to try to bring his ship onto her attack course again. Splinters had pierced some of the steam and hydraulic lines that assisted the helm, and the wheel was desperately heavy to turn. Lieutenant Rettberg ran to help him.

By now, most of the *Cap Trafalgar*'s false bridge was on fire. Steam, smoke, and flames made the *Carmania* difficult to see. The wind blowing strongly over the bows blinded not only those on the bridge but the forward gun crew as well. However, the slight change of course enabled the after gun to get the *Carmania* in its sights, and this opened rapid fire, concentrating on the bridge. Within minutes, the *Carmania*'s bridge was on fire, and as the *Cap Trafalgar* slowly came back onto her course, the wind took the smoke and steam over the starboard quarter, still masking the *Carmania* from the gun crew, but enabling Wirth to see down onto his foredeck.

The forecastle was well alight, but the fire parties seemed to have it in hand. Looking down from the open hatch tops, he could see his boarding parties crouched on their platform while the ammunition men were throwing up shells to Second Officer Schreiner. Through the smoke, though he could not see the *Carmania* herself, he could see the flashes of guns. She had opened the angle between them again so that she could now use her full broadside. Leaving Rettberg to hold the wheel, Wirth went to the bridge rail and shouted down to the foredeck gun crew. "Fire at the gun flashes." Schreiner looked up and acknowledged as he lurched forward with an armful of shells.

A shell from the *Carmania* hit the foremast, ricocheted onto the shield of the forward gun and exploded. A splinter neatly removed Schreiner's head from his body as he went forward. His body continued its momentum, slowly buckling at the knees. Two of the three-man gun crew were badly wounded, the gun itself, jammed at an angle on its mount.

The wind dropped for a moment; Wirth saw that he was about two thousand yards from the *Carmania,* which was still on his starboard bow. Now was the time to make his turn and close. Because of the widening angle, he would have to put his boarders across from the starboard. He shouted to the machine gunners to open up, and, adding his weight to Rettberg's on the wheel, tried to bring his ship head round for the attack. The three starboard machine guns began their vicious chatter. The *Carmania*'s bridge was now untenable. The fire was raging, and the machine-gun bullets compelled the men who were relaying the fire control orders to lie flat on the deck. A burst ripped between Lockyer and Colson, wrecking the rangefinder but leaving them untouched. Both leaped down to the bridge, Lockyer shouting to Grant that it would be prudent to open the range and draw clear of the machine guns.

Grant gave the order to abandon the bridge, and raced down the relatively sheltered port side to the aft control. Barr stayed for a moment, lying flat on the bridge deck as he spoke to the engine room. He ordered, "Full ahead starboard engine, full astern port." The *Carmania* slued to port, presenting her stern quarter to the enemy. As she came through a 90° turn, the wind blew the bridge flames over the bows, and she was able to bring her starboard guns and the aftermost port gun to bear on the *Cap Trafalgar*. Barr still hung on to the engine-room speaking tube, "Steady, full ahead all engines, transferring to aft controls." The bridge and foredeck were now an inferno, and Barr thankfully ran back to rejoin Grant on the stern. The *Cap Trafalgar* was now behind them, and endeavoring to make an equally sharp starboard turn to follow them.

"Do you know," shouted Grant, "I believe the madmen are trying to get alongside."

As the *Carmania* had made her turn, she had also lost ground. The range was now down to almost one thousand yards. Lockyer took in the situation at a glance. He ran down the lines of guns shouting, "Individual fire, aim for the waterline."

A succession of shells smashed into the *Cap Trafalgar*'s waterline at point-blank range. There had been no need even to use the sights; the gunners just squinted along the 4.7-inch barrels.

In the *Cap Trafalgar*'s engine room, Fourth Engineer Adrian Riech could hear nothing of the noise of the battle. The hiss and roar of the machinery deafened him, and he stepped through into the stokehold, where the stokers, bandmen, and singers shifted coal even faster than they had earlier that morning on the two colliers. Riech leaned against the wall by the watertight door serving the two compartments and lit a cigarette. A man hurried past on his way to the ice room, returning a moment later with two buckets of crushed ice, in which the stokers briefly dipped their sweatbands. From habit, Riech spun the bulkhead handle, closing the engine room off from the stokehold.

Seconds later, the *Carmania*'s salvo hit along the starboard side. One shell burst through the skin of the ship, exploding in a coal bunker. Further forward, another exploded where the boiler-room bulkhead met the side of the ship. The bulkhead gave way and water poured through a hole in the side some five feet in diameter. Immediately after another struck in the forward reserve bunker, making a hole about the same size. The stokehold, which was well below the waterline, was awash in seconds. Riech immediately adopted the standard emergency procedure.

This was to flood the port tanks on the opposite side of the ship, in order to create a list and bring the starboard side higher out of the water and reduce the inward flow, then to shut the boilers down, then to try to stop the in-flow, and then to warn other compartments of the ship. He gave the order to flood the port tanks, but kept the boilers going for the time being.

On the bridge, Wirth saw the *Carmania* making her turn. In order to follow her, he decided to use his twin screws to assist him to make a tighter turn. He ordered full ahead port, full astern starboard. His ship responded at once, almost too much he thought, for as her head slowly came round she took a sickening list to starboard.

What had happened was that, as he ordered the starboard turn, the *Cap Trafalgar*'s starboard side was thrust more deeply into the water, increasing the pressure and widening the holes already torn in her plating. Riech struggled to the voice pipe, and shouted to the bridge to make a port turn—otherwise he could not hold the water and the bulkheads would give way. Wirth, who had been unaware of the shots into his hull, had no alternative but to comply.

The *Cap Trafalgar* crabbed slowly to port, again her screws pushing her around. She was now at right angles to the *Carmania*'s stern, and Grant was able to bring first his starboard, then his port broadsides to bear.

Shells landed in the *Cap Trafalgar*'s dining room, starting several fires. Wirth sent Rettberg down to deal with them. The

Carmania had now drawn out of range of his machine guns and he had only his one gun on the stern with which to reply. Slowly he brought the *Cap Trafalgar* further to port, so that now he presented a stern on target. There was still plenty of steam up, so he in turn attempted to open the range in order to try to repair his damage.

It was the end of the first round. The *Carmania* was well on fire forward, and was now heading away from him at full speed, keeping up a steady barrage from the guns on her stern quarters. She was firing four guns to his one, but his rate of fire was considerably higher. Soon she would turn, and by then he would have to have damped his fires and plugged the holes in his waterline; otherwise she would finish him off.

On his present heading, he was facing the wind, and this was blowing the flames down the length of the ship. However, if he turned, then he would be unable to use his stern gun. He compromised, hauling her gently further to port so that the smoke and flame streamed over his port side and partially obscured him from the *Carmania*. Realizing that his boarding parties would no longer be required, he shouted to them to fight the fire and transfer all the ammunition to the after gun.

The *Carmania* headed downwind. The final shots from the *Cap Trafalgar* had shot away the stand-by controls on its afterdeck as well. Now the engine room and rudder were controlled by shouting to a relay of men positioned by the hatches, who in turn shouted down the companionways to the engine room and tiller flat far below. Grant eased her speed so that the *Cap Trafalgar* remained just in range of his 4.7-inch guns and just outside the range of the German's 4.1-inchers. The flames forward were now rising to the height of the funnels, even though the wind was blowing them away from the ship. A messenger ran up to say the main dining room and cabins were on fire beneath the bridge, and that they could not hold it with the men they had. Grant called down to the stokehold for them to send up every available man and, placing Barr in charge of them, sent him forward to take charge of the fire parties.

It was 1 P.M. For almost an hour and a half the two great liners had been hurling everything they had at each other, at a suicidally short range. The *Carmania* had the advantages that she was not taking water, could harass the enemy with her stern guns, and had a larger crew with which to control the fires raging forward and down below.

Langerhannsz and Collmorgen had heard the *Carmania's* first shot. Then for some ten minutes they listened to the roar of the guns as they echoed across the water. It was easy to distinguish whose guns were which. Both ships were visible on the skyline. Langerhannsz watched them close in toward each other, and from his angle of view it seemed to him that they had come together. Moments later the two distant shapes separated, the *Carmania* disappearing behind the island, the *Cap Trafalgar* turning to the north, with smoke pouring from her upperworks. Langerhannsz looked at Collmorgen, who looked back at him, then picked up the voice pipe to the engine room. The *Eleonore Wouvermans* came about, slowly worked up to her maximum speed, and headed toward the sound of the guns.

Langerhannsz felt in his pocket for his cigar case and opened it; he had three left. He reckoned he would need to keep one for what he had in mind. He selected two, sniffed them, rolled them gently in his fingers, peeled off the bands and lit them both. He handed one to Collmorgen and then smoked his fiercely as they steamed into the plume of smoke that the wind blew toward them from the burning *Cap Trafalgar*.

While Barr led the fire parties below, Grant realized that he had neither compass, charts, radio, nor any other navigational instruments with which to extricate his ship from its predicament. He asked for volunteers to try to salvage the compasses from the bridge. Midshipman Colson and Dickens offered to try.

The deck water mains had been shot away, so it was impossible to try to damp the fire down until fresh ones could be rigged. Holding cloths over their faces the two boys plunged into the flames. The compass had to be unscrewed from the binnacle, and they took it in turns to stand in the flames for a moment, each time trying to loosen the retaining screws by a twist or two. Eventually, at the cost of badly burned hands and faces, they were successful. Grant placed the compass on a camp stool beside him on the stern and guided the ship from there.

Below, the water mains were shot through as well, and even if they had been operating, much of the hose was riddled with splinters. Barr tried to damp down the fire by closing off all ventilation, and beating the fire out with the stokers' shovels. He was just beginning to make a little progress, when suddenly the flames burst into new life, racing down the passages between the cabins, licking hungrily at the paint-work. Barr realized that either the wind had shifted or the *Carmania* had changed her heading. At that moment he heard the roar of the guns again. He ran up on deck to find out what was going on.

Grant had turned the *Carmania* and was heading directly for the *Cap Trafalgar*. His guns were back in action but the flames from the bridge were now towering over the funnels and threatening to sweep down to the stern. When Barr had shut ventilators down below in his effort to starve the fire of oxygen, Grant had supposed that he had it under control and had tried to renew his attack. His reason became known when Barr shouted at him, "What the hell are you doing?"

"I am going to take that ship," Grant shouted, pointing his arm. Barr looked.

Chugging placidly in the gap that separated the two liners was the collier *Eleonore Wouvermans.* She was a cable's length away from the *Cap Trafalgar,* and seemed to be heading, not alongside her consort, but upwind of her. As she slogged into position, the *Carmania*'s shells splashed into the water all around. The lone gun on the *Cap Trafalgar* started firing again, punching two shells into Grant's cabin. The gunner then shifted his aim and blew the *Carmania*'s aft anchor winch to pieces.

The *Eleonore Wouvermans* was now slightly beyond the *Cap Trafalgar.* Slowly and fussily she began to turn a full circle so that she appeared to be about to offer an encore and make another pass between the two ships. Collmorgen stood on the bridge, balancing his boat on her helm, while he brought her so that she was facing exactly downwind, with the *Carmania* on her port bow and the *Cap Trafalgar* to starboard.

Langerhannsz, a cigar firmly clamped in his mouth, stood on the jump ladder leading from the main deck up to the foredeck. One hand was hooked around the rungs so as to give himself a purchase; his other held the end of the fuse. He puffed a lungful of smoke into the wind and carefully watched the way the wind carried it. Satisfied, he touched the fuse to the end of his cigar, made sure it was burning, then ducked his head below the level of the foredeck.

There was a blast that drowned the steady thunder of the *Carmania*'s guns, which were still firing. A vast sheet of flame leaped up from the mortar, turning rapidly to dense black smoke that continued to burn as the anthracite chips floated on the swell. A dense smokescreen blanketed the *Cap Trafalgar,* momentarily hiding her from the *Carmania*'s guns.

Jerking his engines hard astern, Collmorgen inched his ship backward and disappeared behind the *Cap Trafalgar*'s hull. Langerhannsz placed his cigar securely in his cap band, which he laid on the deck. He commenced to reload.

🎵

Captain Wirth hung on to the helm. The *Cap Trafalgar* was now hove to. A shell burst among the party fighting the fire in the dining room had killed Chef Sommer, and severely wounded several others, including Rettberg, who had a thigh and a knee shattered and a jagged splinter in his back. A stretcher party brought him out and laid him on the bridge deck beside the captain. Moments later Feddersen reported to the bridge that they could not contain the water in the stokehold. It was only a question of time before it reached the boilers. Wirth asked how the fire was going, but there was really no need for the question. Forward of the bridge, the deck plates glowed almost red hot with the heat from the fire below. Handing over the helm to Feddersen, Wirth knelt by Rettberg, murmuring a few words of comfort. Then he straightened and looked over the splintered bridge rail toward the *Carmania.*

As he did so, a shell struck the superstructure below him, the blast hurling him backward against the helm. Feddersen grabbed to steady him, and noticed a jagged piece of the bridge rail embedded firmly in his left armpit. He dared not remove it, for blood was already pulsing out around the edges of the wound. Wirth found his voice. He ordered Fedderson to clear all men from below and prepare to abandon ship. Then he was to personally explode the blasting charges on the keel and report to him that this scuttling procedure had been carried out. No officer was to leave the ship until the crew were into the boats. Feddersen saluted and began to struggle down to the engine room, shouting on his way, "Abandon ship."

In the boiler room Fourth Engineer Riech dared not open the watertight bulkhead leading through to the engine room. It was the obvious escape route, but the water might cause the boiler to explode. The voice pipe was dead now so he gave the orders for the crew to scramble up the escape ladders to the deck above. He emerged on the stern deck, just below the stern gun, where Lieutenant Klevitz was busy trying to ease the gun, which had jammed. Klevitz called to him to give him a hand. Riech climbed up to the boat deck. The stokers, following their officer's lead, climbed after him. They were still swarming around the gun when they heard the instructions to lower the boats. Once the boats were away, Klevitz was told, officers were to report to the bridge.

By now the *Cap Trafalgar* was listing so far over to starboard that her decks were almost awash. There had been little need to detonate the charges on her keel, but nevertheless Wirth's orders had been carried out. Most of the sixteen boats had been shot to pieces in the battle, but three that were serviceable were loaded. As the *Cap Trafalgar*'s list increased, some men leaped into the water. The *Eleonore Wouvermans,* again bustling around like a mother hen shepherding her chickens, placed herself between the now doomed ship and the *Carmania.* Collmorgen lowered his own boats, which started to pick up the swimmers.

Barr, unaware that his fire-fighting crew had followed him out onto the deck, watched the *Eleonore Wouvermans*'s tactics closely. Forgetting both his dignity and his rank, he shouted to Grant at the top of his voice. What he actually said was never officially recorded. Grant does not mention it in his official report. In a memorandum for his family, which he wrote at the age of eighty, Barr claims he said "in level tones": "You will surely lose this one if you don't keep away."

There was a silence, a quite uncanny silence on the deck of the *Carmania.* In the Royal Navy no one ever challenges the authority of the captain. Men looked first at Barr, then at Grant. The gun crews, suddenly aware that they were committing some kind of solecism by continuing fire, ceased firing one by one. Barr was not pleading for the *Cap Trafalgar,* or for the *Eleonore Wouvermans,* he was fighting for *Car-*

mania, his ship, and every man on the *Carmania*'s deck knew it. To Barr, it was obvious that the *Cap Trafalgar* was doomed, that the *Eleonore Wouvermans* was on a rescue mission, and that to continue upwind would burn the *Carmania* to ashes.

Quietly Grant gave the order to go about. He walked over to Barr and remarked, "Let's get that fire out then." He knelt and shouted down the hatch for half speed ahead. The *Carmania* for the last time pulled out of range.

The *Cap Trafalgar*'s officers ensured that all men, including the wounded, were off the ship. By now, she was lying almost horizontal on her starboard side, her forepeak already under water. The boats, already overloaded, ringed her at a distance of about a hundred yards; those from the *Eleonore Wouvermans* moved quickly among the men in the water. Some charitable soul had released the pigs from the stern-deck pen, and they too had taken to the water. They were swimming strongly in the direction of the island when the first sharks took them; moments later the sharks snatched a swimmer, seconds before he would have been hauled onto a lifeboat. Then another and another; the blood attracted others, and before the last man was hauled aboard, the sea between the *Cap Trafalgar* and the little flotilla of boats was a maelstrom as the sharks, cheated of a meal, began to fight among themselves.

On the bridge, Wirth faced those of his officers who had joined him. There was Feddersen, grimy, capless, tears running down his cheeks. Klevitz was also crying unashamedly. Little Fritz Finke was comforting Erwin Rettberg. Lieutenant Otto Steffan, the *Eber*'s navigator, held a dressing against Wirth's side. Wirth asked him to help him down the now steeply sloping bridge to the starboard side, where the water lapped only a few feet below them.

"Otto," said Wirth, "you always had a strong voice. Call for three cheers for the Kaiser." Otto Steffan raised his voice and shouted across the water. Then, taking off his cap, he led the cheering from the surrounding boats. Wirth turned to his officers. He asked them to tie a life jacket to Rettberg and then to look after themselves. Feddersen obeyed the order, and as he began to drag Rettberg to the edge of the bridge, and follow the others into the water, someone in the boats began to sing.

No one knows who started it. Probably one of the opera singers in one or other of the boats. Feddersen recalled a clear tenor voice rising across the water with the first verse of "the flag song." Then another and another began to sing. The crew on the deck of the *Eleonore Wouvermans* joined in. Langerhannsz standing beside his mortar and Collmorgen on his bridge took up the lilting beat. Soon there were some three hundred voices singing and mentally wishing well to Captain Wirth and the ship. Of that, no one had any doubt. "It was not pride," wrote Langerhannsz, "it was not relief or reaction from battle—we were saying good-bye."

As if in answer to the music, the *Cap Trafalgar* began to recover from her list. Slowly she regained an even keel, and imperceptibly at first began to settle at the bow. Wirth stood on the bridge, leaning against the wheel. Feddersen supported himself on the shattered bridge rail with Rettberg's unconscious body over his shoulder. Then, without warning, the *Cap Trafalgar* lifted her stern high in the air, and with hardly a sound slipped down and out of sight.

Fritz Langerhannsz choked back his tears. He groped blindly in his case for his last cigar. Even the sight of the *Carmania,* blazing merrily on the skyline, was no compensation. His eye fell on his mortar, still smoldering wickedly from the new lease on life he had given it less than an hour before. His anger against the stupidity and waste of what he had witnessed overwhelmed him. Calling for help, he summoned half a dozen of the collier's seamen. With a mighty effort, they up-ended the platform, balanced it on the edge of the foredeck, and then sent it plunging down to join the *Cap Trafalgar*. Then, crying like a child, he allowed Captain Collmorgen to lead him below.

⤷ *Epilogue* ⤶

The *Eleonore Wouvermans* moved closer to search for survivors. She found Feddersen and Rettberg alive and brought them aboard as quickly as possible. Rettberg's left leg was almost completely severed at the knee. Dr. Violet, the *Eber*'s surgeon, who had been rescued himself a few minutes earlier, amputated it on the spot, an ordeal for both men, as the *Eleonore Wouvermans* had neither a doctor nor medical equipment aboard. Lieutenant Erwin Rettberg survived and later, from internment, wrote a full report of the action, which has been accepted by German naval historians as authoritative, Rettberg being the senior surviving officer. Lieutenant Feddersen wrote a report for the directors of the Hamburg South America Line, which covered the period from the outbreak of war until the *Eleonore Wouvermans'* return to Buenos Aires after the action. He differs from Rettberg only insofar as he modestly omits to mention that he was with Rettberg when the *Cap Trafalgar* went down.

The body of Captain Julius Wirth was recovered from the water. He is listed in German naval records as having drowned, but Dr. Violet, who performed a primitive autopsy, established that he died from heart failure, probably induced by the splinter in his armpit blocking the supply of blood from the heart. Either the shock of immersion or of trying to swim caused cardiac arrest. Captain Wirth was buried at sea on September 15, 1914, in company with eleven other members of the crew who were either killed in the action or drowned when the ship went down. A further three were listed as missing. They were undoubtedly taken by sharks.

Five men, including Lieutenant Rettberg, were seriously wounded. Sixty-one suffered minor wounds that required medical attention.

Captain Collmorgen decided, after consultation with Langerhannsz and Feddersen, to make for Buenos Aires. After a ten-day passage, they safely eluded the British blockade of the Plata estuary and landed 286 survivors from the sinking of the *Cap Trafalgar* and 6 former members of her crew, including Langerhannsz, who for one reason or another were on board the *Eleonore Wouvermans* at the time.

The survivors were interned for the duration of the war on the island of Martin Barcia, which lies in the Plata estuary.

Commander Langerhannsz handed Captain Wirth's war diary and papers to Captain Collmorgen to pass on to the German authorities. Collmorgen made an accurate copy of it, handing the original to the German Legation in Buenos Aires, and retained the copy, which he intended to hand over to the *Dresden.*

The name of the *Eleonore Wouvermans* was changed to *Anna,* and under this name she served as a supply ship and collier to the *Dresden* and *Kronprinz Wilhelm.* On January 6, 1915, she was stopped just north of the Falkland Islands by H.M.S. *Australia,* commanded by Admiral Patey. Captain Collmorgen and his crew were made prisoners and their ship destroyed. Captain Wirth's war diary and Collmorgen's log thus came into British hands.

The *Pontos* was sunk by H.M.S. *Glasgow* during November, 1914, while the *Berwind,* having been the subject of diplomatic protests by England to the United States, ended her days carrying cotton from the port of Charleston to Rotterdam.

The gunboat *Eber* remained anchored off Bahía until October, 1917. Her crew, with the exception of a maintenance team of thirteen men, were interned. On October 26, 1917, after the entry of the United States into the war, an attempt was made to requisition the *Eber* for the Argentinian Navy. The maintenance crew scuttled her where she was anchored, and she lies off Bahía to this day.

Both the *Carmania* and the British Admiralty remained unaware of the identity of the *Cap Trafalgar* until the arrival of the *Eleonore Wouvermans* with the survivors. The *Carmania* had reported engaging a heavily armed auxiliary cruiser, fitted with at least eight guns, in addition to machine guns.

The Argentine and Uruguayan authorities did not believe that the *Cap Trafalgar* had carried only the *Eber*'s two guns and six machine guns, and presumed that Langerhannsz had misled them when he had given his word of honor to the port inspector in Montevideo that the *Cap Trafalgar* was not armed. He was removed to Montevideo to stand trial and was acquitted. His own account, written in Montevideo for the benefit of his defense counsel, was accepted "in toto" by the court. A copy of his evidence was sent through diplomatic channels to Captain Grant and Commander Barr, inviting their comments. They had none to offer, so Langerhannsz's acquittal was due to lack of evidence. The British claim against the Argentine and Uruguayan governments was abandoned by the British Foreign Secretary for similar lack of evidence.

The *Dresden* was eventually cornered by a British battle squadron as she lay anchored in Cumberland Bay off the Chilean coast. She was badly damaged by salvos from the *Kent, Glasgow,* and *Orama.* Captain Lüdecke, unable to escape from the harbor, blew up his ship.

The *Kronprinz Wilhelm* managed to capture and sink more Allied ships and to evade capture. On April 11, 1915, her boilers in need of repair, she voluntarily interned herself at Newport News.

Dr. Braunholz lived in happy isolation until February, 1915, when he was taken aboard the German auxiliary cruiser *Prinz Eitel Friedrich,* which had escaped from the Pacific around the Horn into the Atlantic. After capturing and destroying several Allied ships, machinery problems and lack of supplies caused her to seek internment in the United States. As a civilian, Dr. Braunholz was allowed to land, and from that sanctuary wrote a graphic account of his adventures for the German newspaper *Weser Zeitung.*

The officers and crew of the *Carmania* fought the blaze until nightfall, when they managed to bring it under control. A relief radio was rigged up, and messages were sent for assistance. The following morning the cruiser *Bristol* arrived, sending aboard a party to make temporary repairs.

The *Carmania* suffered casualties of 9 killed and 26 wounded requiring hospitalization. She had neither engine-room nor steering controls, had been hit by 79 shells, and there were 304 holes in her hull and superstructure. Most of her deck machinery, such as winches, derricks, and boats, had been shot to pieces. H.M.S. *Bristol* escorted her to a rendezvous with the *Cornwall* at the Abrolhos Rocks, where after more temporary repairs she was sent in convoy to Gibraltar for repairs at the dockyard there. These took eight weeks. Thereafter she was employed as a patrol vessel operating off Lisbon. After the war she returned to Liverpool, was refurbished as a passenger liner, and became a popular choice with transatlantic travelers until she was broken up in 1925.

Captain Noel Grant continued in command for a short period, but the increasing periods of hospitalization resulted in his being declared medically unfit for further sea service in

February, 1916. He had been awarded the decoration of Commander of the Bath (military division) by the King in June, 1915, and assumed command of a shore establishment. He was promoted to Rear Admiral on January 27, 1920. He retired from the Navy at his own request the following day and died of tuberculosis five weeks later on March 6.

Commander James Barr was granted sick leave in January, 1915, shortly after the *Carmania* took up her patrol duties off Lisbon. He was invalided home and found to be medically unfit for further sea duty with the Royal Navy. He too was awarded the C.B. for his services. He returned to Cunard. He commanded the *Mauretania, Saxonia,* and *Carpathia,* all in use as troop ships making passages to Canada, Australia, India, and the Dardanelles, until he retired as Senior Commodore of the line in 1916. He died at the age of eighty-two on March 30, 1937.

Lieutenant Commander Lockyer was awarded the Distinguished Service Order, and returned to his interrupted retirement after a spell on patrol off Lisbon.

All the officers of the *Carmania* were Mentioned in Despatches * except Surgeon Edwin Maynard and Lieutenant Battle of the R.N.R. Both returned to the Cunard Company and wrote their own accounts of the voyage and action, which their descendants have passed to the author. Lieutenant Battle also wrote a small booklet, which was published by Cunard on the occasion of a remarkable ceremony held aboard the *Carmania* on September 15, 1919.

In 1919, a civilian body called The Navy League acquired twenty-four silver plates that were originally the property of Lord Nelson and which had been with him aboard H.M.S. *Victory* at Trafalgar. The league decided to present a plate to selected ships of the Royal Navy that had rendered outstand-

---

* A minor honor in the British armed forces, rating below a medal.

ing service during the war. The *Carmania* was the only civilian ship so honored. The plate hung in her main saloon as a tribute to men of the merchant service, and as a memento of Nelson. There can be little doubt that Commander Langerhannsz would have approved.

There were two other sequels. Captain Grant, who knew his naval regulations better than most, brought an action for "prize money" to be awarded to the officers and crew of the *Carmania* under centuries-old naval law. It was the first case of its kind for generations and was successful. Certain statements as to the *Cap Trafalgar*'s armament and the size of her crew were entered into the court record, and have since formed the basis for the official version of the action. They were made in good faith, but they were seriously inaccurate in that they claim that the *Cap Trafalgar* carried a heavier armament than the *Carmania*. A transcript of the prize court proceedings is given as an appendix.

In 1974, which was the International Geophysical Year, a Brazilian survey party examined the island of Trinidad. They recorded its rainfall, plant and animal life, and its geophysical characteristics. They also noted that it was inhabited by a herd of wild, curiously mottled pigs of a strain that appeared to be peculiar to the island.

❧ *Appendix I* ☙

ADMIRALTY, S.W.,
18th January, 1921.

The following Officers have been mentioned in despatches for
distinguished services rendered during the action between
H.M.S. *Carmania* and the German Armed Merchant Cruiser
Cap Trafalgar on the 14th September, 1914.

> Cdr. James Barr, R.N.R.
> Lieut-Cdr. Edmund Laurence Braithwaite Lockyer, R.N.
> Lieut-Cdr. William James O'Neill, R.N.R.
> Chief Eng. Francis Drummond, R.N.R.
> Lieut. Peter Archibald Murchie, R.N.R.
> Senior Eng. James Macdonald, R.N.R.
> Act. Sub-Lieut. George Frederick Dickens, R.N.R.
> Mid. Douglas Nowell Colson, R.N.R.
> Chief Gnr. Henry Middleton, R.N.

⋑ *Appendix II* ⋐

IN THE HIGH COURT OF JUSTICE
PROBATE DIVORCE & ADMIRALTY DIVN.
(ADMIRALTY)
IN PRIZE.
27th March 1916

H.M.S. "C A R M A N I A"

SHORTHAND NOTES

> Treasure Solicitor,
> Law Courts Branch,
> 276 Royal Courts of Justice
> Strand, W.C.

IN THE HIGH COURT OF JUSTICE
PROBATE DIVORCE & ADMIRALTY DIVISION
A D M I R A L T Y.
I N P R I Z E.

Monday, 27th March 1916.

BEFORE:—

The Right Hon: Sɪʀ Sᴀᴍᴜᴇʟ Eᴠᴀɴs

President.

*   *   *

H.M.S. "C A R M A N I A"

(A Motion in respect of a claim for Prize Bounty).

Cᴏᴍᴍᴀɴᴅᴇʀ Mᴀxᴡᴇʟʟ H. Aɴᴅᴇʀsᴏɴ appeared for the
Captain and Ship's Company.

Mʀ. R. C. Dᴜɴʟᴏᴘ appeared for the Procurator General
on behalf of the Crown.

*

Cᴏᴍᴍᴀɴᴅᴇʀ Mᴀxᴡᴇʟʟ H. Aɴᴅᴇʀsᴏɴ: May it please your
Lordship, in this case I appear for the Captain and Ship's
Company of H.M. Ship *Carmania* to move your Lordship to
declare that they are entitled to prize bounty as being actually
present at the time of the destruction to an enemy of His
Majesty, to wit, the German Emperor, and that there were at
the beginning of the engagement on board the said enemy
ship, 437 persons and that the amount of prize money
calculated at the rate of £5 per head is £2185.

Tʜᴇ Pʀᴇsɪᴅᴇɴᴛ: Where do you get the £5 per head from?

Cᴏᴍᴍᴀɴᴅᴇʀ Aɴᴅᴇʀsᴏɴ: The Order in Council.

Tʜᴇ Pʀᴇsɪᴅᴇɴᴛ: You are going to call my attention to it.

Cᴏᴍᴍᴀɴᴅᴇʀ Aɴᴅᴇʀsᴏɴ: I am going to call your Lordship's attention to it. My learned friend, Mr. Dunlop, I
understand, appears on behalf of the Crown, not so much to
resist the amount as to check any tendency to excessive
generosity on the part of the Court. As this is the first case of
its kind in the present war, my Lord, it might be convenient to

your Lordship if I sketched out the history of this head money. It is a grant from the Crown provided out of monies supplied by Parliament as a personal reward for the sinking or capture of an armed vessel belonging to the enemy forces. In the earlier days when vessels of the Royal Navy and the Mercantile Marine were not very dissimilar in construction or design, it was more or less customary to give prize money to the captors; but in the time of the Commonwealth it was decided that some special reward should be given to those who by personal exertion destroyed an armed ship—a recognized armed ship in the Government employ of the enemy and by caput 21 of the year 1649 it was enacted that for all enemy ships of war, burnt, sunk, or destroyed, there should be paid, for an Admiral's ship £20 per gun, for a Vice Admiral's ship £16 per gun, and for an ordinary ship of war £10 per gun.

THE PRESIDENT: I observe you did not give the regnal year—was it in the reign of Charles I or during the Commonwealth?

COMMANDER ANDERSON: Charles I according to the practice in this country reigned down to 1660, and the year I have given is 1649 which is near enough.

THE PRESIDENT: You will not get a citation of an Act of Parliament in any year of the Commonwealth—I do not know why.

COMMANDER ANDERSON: At this time the captors were allowed the pillage or plunder of anything above the gun deck; but this led to lawlessness and accordingly by the 4th and 5th William and Mary Chapter 21, in lieu of plunder the captors were given a definite share in the proceeds of prize, and in addition for a war ship £10 per gun. But on account of the complaints which were very frequent at that time as to the low rates of pay to and lack of encouragement of Naval Officers, pamphlets were circulated showing the advantages of serving in the French Navy as opposed to the British Navy,

and as the result of that agitation the first Prize Act, which is
Anne, Chapter 13, was passed, and by section 8 of that Act, it
was enacted, that with a view to encouraging the capture of
ships of war belonging to the enemy, if in any action any ship
of war or privateer shall be taken from the enemy, £5 shall be
granted to the captor for every gun which was on board such
ship or ships so taken at the beginning of the engagement
between them. It was felt later that this was too restrictive, as
that section required the ship to be literally taken and brought
in. That was put right by the Act of 45 George III Chapter 72,
in which it was enacted that the bounty might be paid for the
taking, sinking or destroying or burning of the ship. Those
grants have been renewed in every subsequent war almost,
and by virtue of section 42 of the present Naval Prize Act of
1864. His Majesty by an Order in Council of the 2nd of March
1915 declared his intention to grant bounty to the officers and
crews of such of his ships of war as are actually present at the
taking or destroying of any armed ship of any of his Majesty's
enemies, and there shall be distributed amongst them as prize
bounty, grants of a sum calculated at the rate of £5 for each
person on board the enemy's ship at the beginning of the
engagement.

THE PRESIDENT: Does this prize bounty come from the
Prize Fund?

COMMANDER ANDERSON: No, my Lord, this is from money
provided by Parliament. In order to get that money, my Lord,
the claimants have come to your Lordship for a decree that
they are the sole and proper persons to receive the bounty,
and it is also for your Lordship, after hearing the evidence to
declare the number of men on board the enemy's ship at the
commencement of the engagement.

THE PRESIDENT: Yes.

COMMANDER ANDERSON: This case is not contested in any

way between the parties claiming the bounty. It is a case of a single ship action.

THE PRESIDENT: No joint claim.

COMMANDER ANDERSON: No joint captors' claim. It may be of interest to notice from the old cases of joint captors, where various ships' companies have come before the Court for a decision as to who is the rightful person to have the bounty, that the Court has been assisted by the Elder Brethren of Trinity House as Assessors—that was so in the case of the *Varsovie,* reported in 2 Dodson page 301. In looking back through the cases of 100 years ago, there are certain rules which can be found amongst them and the first is that the actual destruction or surrender of the enemy's ship is a necessity. That is decided in *La Clorinde* 1 Dodson 439. An actual fight is not required, but the enemy may be induced to surrender by the overpowering force in front of him. In this case the facts are very short and simple. The *Carmania* was one of a number of merchant ships requisitioned for the use of the Crown on the outbreak of war in 1914. She was armed and converted into an auxiliary cruiser commanded by an Officer of the Royal Navy holding his Majesty's commission, and thereupon she became a public ship and an integral portion of the naval forces. She was placed under the command of Captain Noel Grant, who claims a share on behalf of himself and the ship's company. On September 14th, 1914 while at sea, she encountered the German vessel the *Cap Trafalgar* which was enjoying exactly a similar status under the German Emperor, that is to say, the *Cap Trafalgar* was a Hamburg Amerika Liner, and was in a similar commission under circumstances which I will make a little plainer to your Lordship in a moment. The evidence has been prepared by an affidavit, because it was not known whether Captain Grant would be present here today and by Order 33 rule 4 the admission of evidence on affidavit is permissible; but Captain Grant is present in Court today and if your Lordship would prefer his going into the witness box to my reading the affidavit he will do so.

THE PRESIDENT: As you please.

COMMANDER ANDERSON: I will read the affidavit. It is an affidavit by Noel Grant, Commander of the most honourable Order of the Bath.

THE PRESIDENT: The affidavit I believe, strictly speaking, ought not to be used except where the officer is not available— is not that the first part of the rule, that the witnesses shall be heard before the Judge in a Court and then it goes on alternatively to provide that their evidence may be given on affidavit.

COMMANDER ANDERSON: If your Lordship pleases.

THE PRESIDENT: Very well.

CAPTAIN NOEL GRANT sworn:

EXAMINED BY COMMANDER MAXWELL H. ANDERSON

Q. Are you Captain Noel Grant in the Royal Navy?

A. Yes.

Q. Were you recently in command of H.M. Ship *Carmania*?

A. Yes.

Q. Were you in command of her on the 14th September 1914?

A. Yes.

Q. What were you doing on that date?

A. Do you want me to give a detailed account of what happened?

THE PRESIDENT: Give us a short descriptive account.

COMMANDER ANDERSON: You were at sea cruising, were not you?

A. Yes.

THE PRESIDENT: Will the Captain please tell us?

CAPTAIN GRANT: About half past 9 in the morning on September 14th, we sighted the *Cap Trafalgar*. We did not know she was the *Cap Trafalgar* then of course. She was coaling and there were two other colliers with her. When she saw us she stopped coaling and apparently steamed away. We went after her. Then she turned and I fired across her bows. She opened fire and the firing then became general. We manoeuvred a little bit and she eventually went away steaming away from us with a heavy list to starboard. We chased her.

THE PRESIDENT: You had hit her, I suppose?

CAPTAIN GRANT: Yes, she was badly hit, we were badly hit too at that time.

THE PRESIDENT: You chased her.

CAPTAIN GRANT: We chased her. We chased her to leeward. Both ships being very badly on fire, we had to go to leeward to prevent the flames from spreading too much. She had the speed of me and was getting out of gun range, but eventually she turned 16 points, turned over and went down.

THE PRESIDENT: What was the distance between the two vessels at that time about?

CAPTAIN GRANT: We opened fire at 8000 yards and got down to about 2800 and then I turned away from her, because she had machine guns which we had not, and also I hoped that she would follow me round, because if I got her on my quarter I could fight 5 guns instead of 4. But she would not follow me. She followed me a little way and turned off to the southward and I had to make a complete turn to the southward and go after her; so that increased the distance between the two ships to about 10,000 yards, and at the end of the action, when she went down she was outside of range altogether and she must have been 10,000 yards off.

THE PRESIDENT: How long approximately did the action last?

CAPTAIN GRANT: The action lasted about one hour and

three quarters from the time the first shot was fired until she went over.

COMMANDER ANDERSON: During the time you were in action, the vessel was flying the war flag of the German Navy.

CAPTAIN GRANT: She went down with her colours flying.

Q. She sank with her colours flying.

A. Yes.

THE PRESIDENT: What colours was she flying when you first sighted her?

A. That I cannot say, she was too far distant.

COMMANDER ANDERSON: Do you know where she received her armament?

A. No, only by hearsay—I do not know at all otherwise.

Q. And you have no personal knowledge of the number of people on board the *Cap Trafalgar* at the beginning of the action?

A. No, I have no personal knowledge.

COMMANDER ANDERSON: I have an affidavit by Sir William Graham Greene.

THE PRESIDENT: Do you not think you ought to ask Captain Grant about paragraph 10?

COMMANDER ANDERSON: That is in the Secretary to the Admiralty's affidavit.

THE PRESIDENT: Is it?

COMMANDER ANDERSON: Yes and Captain Grant does not know that of his own personal knowledge.

THE PRESIDENT: He says "he is informed and believes." He had got it from someone else I suppose. (To the Witness). You say in your affidavit, Captain Grant, that you are informed and believe that the *Cap Trafalgar* met at sea the German war vessel *Eber* and that the Officer of the *Eber* took command of the *Cap Trafalgar* and that the *Cap Trafalgar* was at the time of the action duly commissioned as an auxiliary cruiser to the Imperial German Navy. Where does that information come from?

CAPTAIN GRANT: My Lord, I had no information as to where she got her people from. In fact, I had no information that they were naval men on board at all to my own knowledge.

THE PRESIDENT: You have got the information from someone apparently.

MR. DUNLOP: From the Secretary of the Admiralty—your Lordship will see it in the affidavit.

THE PRESIDENT: Very well, thank you.

COMMANDER ANDERSON: The following is the affidavit of Sir William Graham Greene, K.C.B., Secretary of the Admiralty:—"The British auxiliary cruiser *Carmania,* Captain Noel Grant, R.N., went into action on Sept. 14, 1914, off the east coast of South America with a German armed merchant cruiser, the *Cap Trafalgar,* mounting eight 4 in. guns and pompoms. The action lasted 1 hour and 45 minutes, then the German ship capsized and sank, her survivors being rescued by an empty collier. Of the crew of the *Carmania* nine men were killed, five men seriously injured, and 21 men slightly wounded. The *Cap Trafalgar* was a Hamburg-America Line vessel, of 18,710 tons gross, built in 1913. At the outbreak of the war the *Cap Trafalgar* was fitted out as an auxiliary cruiser at Buenos Ayres, and I am informed, and verily believe, that the *Cap Trafalgar* at some time prior to Sept. 14, 1914 met at sea with the German warship *Eber* from which she obtained her armament, together with officers and crews for the guns. It is not possible to state with absolute accuracy the number of persons on board the *Cap Trafalgar* at the time of the action with H.M.S. *Carmania.* From enquiries which I have caused to be made I have ascertained that the peace complement of the *Cap Trafalgar* would have been about 350 men and the war complement about 400 men. With special reference to the amount of prize bounty awardable to the ship's company of the *Carmania,* special inquiry has been made by His Majesty's Minister at Buenos Ayres, and I am informed and verily believe that the *Cap Trafalgar* was despatched from Buenos Ayres on August 7th 1914 with a crew of 423 all told, and that a fighting crew was substituted for the merchant crew at some date prior to Sept 14th 1914, but no details were available as to number. Further inquiries have been made by His Britannic Majesty's Consul at Bahia, where the crew of the warship *Eber* is interned, who reports that the *Cap Trafalgar* had on board 392 persons. I therefore believe that there were on board the *Cap Trafalgar* at the time the action commenced not less than 392 persons, and not more than 423 persons."

THE PRESIDENT: Where does he get the 423 from?

COMMANDER ANDERSON: He gets that from His Majesty's Minister at Buenos Ayres.

THE PRESIDENT: That she had a crew at Buenos Ayres of 423?

COMMANDER ANDERSON: Yes.

THE PRESIDENT: Where do you get your 437 from?

COMMANDER ANDERSON: I am now going to read that—it is in a short affidavit by the Collector of Customs and Excise at Southampton, Henry William Veale, who says—"The Hamburg-America liner *Cap Trafalgar* was before the war a regular calling vessel at the port of Southampton. From the records concerning the granting of clearance to the ship *Cap Trafalgar* which records have been made in due course of law and are in my custody, I find that the *Cap Trafalgar* last cleared from the port of Southampton on July 16, 1914, and she then had a crew of 439 persons. On the voyage immediately preceding the one referred to the *Cap Trafalgar* cleared from the port of Southampton on June 29, 1914, and she then had a crew of 437 persons." So that the numbers vary from 392, the minimum by the Admiralty, to 437, the crew she had when she left Southampton on the voyage from which she never returned.

THE PRESIDENT: On the 16th of July?

COMMANDER ANDERSON: On the 16th July.

THE PRESIDENT: Have you had any means of ascertaining whether that crew was the crew of a merchant ship or not?

COMMANDER ANDERSON: No, my Lord. There is no reason to believe that it was other than a purely mercantile crew.

THE PRESIDENT: An ordinary crew.

COMMANDER ANDERSON: Yes, my Lord.

THE PRESIDENT: Is there any evidence before me as to whether the Naval crew was likely to exceed in numbers the ordinary crew?

COMMANDER ANDERSON: Well my Lord, no, it is rather to the contrary I am afraid. The Secretary of the Admiralty you will remember says that he was informed that her war complement would be about 400, although he goes on to say that there might have been a maximum of 423.

THE PRESIDENT: I am inclined to give you the maximum that I ought according to the evidence to give—what do you say that is?

COMMANDER ANDERSON:The maximum according to the evidence, my Lord, would be 437, but 423 we might justly have, my Lord. It had got to be divided amongst a large number.

THE PRESIDENT: Yes, I have already told you that the inclination either of my mind or of my heart is to give you as much as I can.

COMMANDER ANDERSON: The Treasury also take 5 per cent before the recipients get it.

THE PRESIDENT: The Treasury are a hard Department.

COMMANDER ANDERSON: I submit that the 423 is a very fair figure.

MR. DUNLOP: Might I supplement the interesting observations which my learned friend made with regard to the history of the Bounty Legislation by referring your Lordship to those sections which deal with the law as it stands at present—

Sections 42, 43 and 44 of the Naval Prize Act?

THE PRESIDENT: I have got them before me.

MR. DUNLOP: The Order in Council is in Supplement 3 of the Emergency Manual at page 499. The Order in Council of the 2nd March 1915 brings into operation and applies to the present war the provisions of the Naval Prize Act of 1864.

THE PRESIDENT: Yes. Then there is an Order in Council of the 29th February 1916—but does that deal with the matter or does it only deal with the distribution?

MR. DUNLOP: That only deals with the distribution after your Lordship has made the award.

THE PRESIDENT: I have nothing to do with distribution?

MR. DUNLOP: No, my Lord, your Lordship has nothing to do with distribution. The only matter is with regard to the procedure and your Lordship will see the form of degree in the Manual.

THE PRESIDENT: Yes, I have read that. That is No. 25 of Order 33.

MR. DUNLOP: No. 25.

COMMANDER ANDERSON: There is one other point to bring before your Lordship in making the decree—the 2½ per cent for the Naval Agents. That is dealt with in Section 19 of the Naval Distribution Prize Agency Act of 1864 which provides that before any such money as aforesaid is distributed among the officers and crew there shall be paid under the direction of the Lords of the Admiralty to the ship's Agent a percentage of £2.10.0 per cent.

THE PRESIDENT: I have nothing to do with that—so far as I am concerned you shall have the gross amount. Mr. Dunlop what do you say about the number?

MR. DUNLOP: Your Lordship had the evidence and I assent to what your Lordship intimates.

THE PRESIDENT: What do you say?

Mr. Dunlop: 423.

The President: The average between 423 and 392 is 415.

Mr. Dunlop: Yes, your Lordship has the evidence, and I have heard what your Lordship has said.

JUDGEMENT

The President: By the Act of 1864, Section 42, a prize bounty of a sum calculated at the rate of £5 for each of the persons on board the enemy's ship at the beginning of an engagement can be awarded to the officers and crew of any of His Majesty's ships of war who were actually present at the taking or destroying of any armed ship of an enemy, and it appears from the evidence before me that the officers and crew who are the claimants here were present at the destruction of an armed ship of the German Empire, to wit, the *Cap Trafalgar* on the date spoken to. The number of persons on board cannot be proved to an exact figure, because the *Cap Trafalgar* was sunk in the fight. I am allowed to ascertain the number so as to get the figure on which to calculate the amount of prize bounty upon such evidence as may seem to me sufficient in the circumstances. I find that the number of persons upon the enemy's ship should be regarded for this purpose as 423. The prize bounty therefore will be the sum of £2115 and I pronounce and declare that the Applicants, namely, the officers and crew of His Majesty's Ship *Carmania* of which Captain Noel Grant was the commander, are entitled to that prize bounty as being actually present at the destruction of the *Cap Trafalgar*, and that the amount of the prize money is the sum of £2115.

205

IN PRIZE
> In the matter of H. M. S. CARMANIA
> *Prize Bounty.*

Copy

D E C R E E

> *Treasury Solicitor,*
> *276 Royal Courts of Justice,*
> *Strand W. C.*

IN THE HIGH COURT OF JUSTICE
PROBATE DIVORCE & ADMIRALTY DIVISION
IN PRIZE
> In the matter of H.M.S. *'CARMANIA'*

Prize Bounty

*

On the 27th day of March 1916.

The President having heard the notice of motion and the evidence thereon, and having heard counsel for the applicants the Officers and Ship's Company of His Majesty's Ship *Carmania* and counsel for the Crown pronounced and declared that the said Officers and Ship's Company of His Majesty's Ship *Carmania*, Noel Grant C.B., Commander, are entitled to prize bounty as being actually present at the destroying of the armed ship *Cap Trafalgar*, belonging at the time of destruction thereof to an enemy of His Majesty, to wit the German Emperor, and that at the beginning of the engagement there were on board the said enemy's ship 423 persons, and that the amount of prize bounty aforesaid is the sum of £2115.